The Britannica Guide to Islam

Islamic Art and Architecture

Edited by Peter Osier

Britannica Educational Publishing

in association with

Rosen Educational Services

Published in 2018 by Britannica Educational Publishing (a trademark of Encyclopædia Britannica, Inc.) in association with The Rosen Publishing Group, Inc.
29 East 21st Street, New York, NY 10010

Distributed exclusively by Rosen Publishing.
To see additional Britannica Educational Publishing titles, go to rosenpublishing.com.

First Edition

Britannica Educational Publishing
J.E. Luebering: Executive Director, Core Editorial
Andrea R. Field: Managing Editor, Compton's by Britannica

Rosen Publishing
Amelie von Zumbusch: Editor
Nelson Sá: Art Director
Brian Garvey: Series Designer
Cindy Reiman: Photography Manager
Nicole DiMella: Photo Researcher

Library of Congress Cataloging-in-Publication Data

Names: Osier, Peter, editor.
Title: Islamic art and architecture / [editor] Peter Osier.
Description: Britannica Educational Publishing : New York, NY, 2018. | Series: The Britannica guide to Islam | Includes bibliographical references and index.
Identifiers: LCCN 2016053714 | ISBN 9781680486131 (library bound : alk. paper)
Subjects: LCSH: Islamic art—History. | Islamic architecture—History.
Classification: LCC N6260 .I822 2018 | DDC 704/.088297—dc23
LC record available at https://lccn.loc.gov/2016053714—

Manufactured in China

Photo credits: Cover, p. 1 Prazis/Shutterstock.com; pp. 6-7 Jesse Durocher/Moment/Getty Images; p. 15 P Deliss/Corbis Documentary/Getty Images; p. 17 Pascal Deloche/Corbis Documentary/Getty Images; p. 27 © semultura/Fotolia; p. 29 Archivo Mas, Barcelona; p. 32 A.F. Kersting; p. 33 Marc Garanger/Corbis Documentary/Getty Images; p. 36 Ryan Rodrick Beiler/Shutterstock.com; p. 42 Matej Kastelic/Shutterstock.com; p. 45 DEA/G. Dagli Orti/DeAgostini/Getty Images; p. 47 Ciccione—Rapho/Photo Researchers; p. 49 De Agostini Picture Library/Getty Images; p. 56 Scott D. Haddow/Moment Open/Getty Images; p. 60 Werner Forman/Universal Images Group/Getty Images; p. 67 JTB Photo/Universal Images Group/Getty Images; p. 68 Roland and Sabrina Michaud—Rapho/Photo Researchers; p. 72 Ara Guler, Istanbul; p. 74 Courtesy of the Bibliothèque Nationale, Paris; pp. 76, 98 Courtesy of the Victoria and Albert Museum, London; photograph John Webb; p. 78 © Rafael Ramirez/Fotolia; p. 83 Michel Setboun/Corbis Documentary/Getty Images; p. 85 Angelo Hornak/Alamy Stock Photo; p. 88 Jupiterimages—Photos.com/Thinkstock; p. 92 Courtesy of the Trustees of the British Library; p. 97 muratart/Shutterstock.com; p. 101 © javarman/Fotolia; p. 103 Courtesy of the Victoria and Albert Museum, London; p. 106 © TMAX/Fotolia; p. 111 P. Chandra; back cover, pp. 3-5 background design javarman/Shutterstock.com; interior pages border design Azat1976/Shutterstock.com

CONTENTS

INTRODUCTION 6

CHAPTER 1
ORIGINS 11
Earlier Artistic Traditions 11
The Mosque 12
The Prohibition Against Images 14
Arabic Script 18

CHAPTER 2
THE EARLY PERIOD 21
Architecture 22
Early Religious Buildings 23
Three Great Mosques 25
Other Classic Mosques 28
Dome of the Rock 30
Other Types of Religious Buildings 31
Secular Architecture 34
Urban Design 39
Building Materials and Technology 40
Architectural Decoration 43

Decorative Arts 47
Assessment 51

CHAPTER 3
MIDDLE PERIOD 53
Fāṭimid Art (909–1171) 54
Architecture 54
Decorative Arts 58
Fāṭimid Book Illustration 59
Seljuq Art 61
Characteristic Architectural Forms 62
Caravansaries 64
Architecture in Iran 65
Architecture in Iraq, Syria, and Anatolia 69
Other Arts 73
Western Islamic Art: Moorish 76
Mamlūk Art 81
Architecture 82
Other Arts 84
Mongol Iran: Il-Khanid and Timurid Periods 86

Architecture 87
Painting 89

CHAPTER 4
LATE PERIOD TO THE PRESENT DAY 94
Ottoman Art 94
Architecture 95
Other Arts 98
Ṣafavid Art 99
Architecture 100
Painting 102
Mughal Art 104
Architecture 105
Painting 107
The Mughal Atelier 109
Islamic Art Under European Influence and Contemporary Trends 113

CONCLUSION 116
GLOSSARY 117
BIBLIOGRAPHY 119
INDEX 126

INTRODUCTION

What, exactly, is Islamic art? When discussing Islamic art, it is first essential to realize that no ethnic group or geographical area was Muslim from the beginning. There is no Islamic art in the way there is a Chinese art or a French art. Nor is it simply a period art, like Gothic art or Baroque art, for once a land or an ethnic entity became Muslim, it remained Muslim (with just a small number of exceptions, such as Spain or Sicily). Political and social events transformed a number of lands with a variety of earlier histories into Muslim lands. But because early Islam as such did not have an artistic style its own, each area could continue, in fact often did continue, whatever modes of creativity it already had acquired. It may then not be appropriate at all to talk about the visual arts of Islamic peoples, and one could instead consider separately each of the areas that became Muslim: Spain, North Africa, Egypt, Syria, Mesopotamia, Iran, Anatolia, and India. Such, in fact, has been the direction taken by some scholarship. Even though tainted at times with parochial nationalism, that approach has been useful in that it has focused attention on a number of permanent features in different regions of Islamic lands that are older than and independent from the faith itself and from the political entity created by it. Iranian art, in particular, exhibits a number of features (cer-

Many of the masterpieces of Islamic architecture are mosques. The Sultan Ahmed Cami, in Istanbul, Turkey, is the work of architect Mehmed Ağa. The design of the mosque—called the Blue Mosque because of the colour of its tile work—is perfectly symmetrical.

tain themes such as the representation of birds or an epic tradition in painting) that owe little to its Islamic character since the 7th century. Ottoman art shares a Mediterranean tradition of architectural conception with Italy rather than with the rest of the Muslim world.

If one looks at the art of Islamic lands from a different perspective, though, a totally different picture emerges. The perspective is that of the lands that surround the Muslim world or of the times that preceded its formation. For even if there are ambiguous examples, most observers can recognize a flavour, a mood in Islamic visual arts that is distinguishable from what is known in East Asia (China, Korea, and Japan) or in the Christian West. This mood or flavor has been called decorative, for it seems at first glance to emphasize an immense complexity of surface effects without apparent meanings attached to the visible motifs. But it has other characteristics as well: it is often colourful, both in architecture and in objects; it avoids representations of living things; it gives much prominence to the work of artisans and counts among its masterpieces not merely works of architecture or of painting but also the creations of weavers, potters, and metalworkers. The problem is whether these uniquenesses of Islamic art, when compared with other artistic traditions, are the result of the nature of Islam or of some other factor or series of factors.

Each artistic tradition has tended to develop its own favourite mediums and techniques. Some, such as architecture, are automatic needs of every culture, and it is in the medium of architecture that some of the most characteristically Islamic works of art are found. Other techniques have different degrees of importance in different traditions. Sculpture in the round hardly existed as a major art form in the Islamic world, while wall painting existed but has generally been poorly preserved. The great Islamic art of painting was the illustration of books. The unique feature of Islamic techniques is the astounding development taken by the decorative arts—such as woodwork, glass, ceramics, metalwork, and textiles. New techniques were invented and spread throughout the Muslim world—at times even beyond its frontiers. In dealing with Islam, therefore, it is quite incorrect to think of those techniques as the "minor" arts, for the amount and intensity of creative energies spent on the decorative arts transformed them into major artistic forms, and their significance in defining a profile of the aesthetic and visual language of Islamic peoples is far greater than in the instances of many other cultures. Furthermore, because, for a variety of reasons to be discussed later, the Muslim world did not develop until quite late the notion of "noble" arts, the decorative arts have reflected far better the needs and ambitions of the culture as a whole. The kind of conclusion that can be reached about Islamic civilization through its visual arts thus extends far deeper than is usual in the study of an artistic tradition, and it requires a combination of archaeological, art-historical, and textual information.

An example may suffice to demonstrate the point. Among all the techniques of Islamic visual arts, the most important one was the art of textiles. Textiles, of course, were used for daily wear at all social levels and for all occasions. But clothes were also the main indicators of rank, and they were given as rewards or as souvenirs by princes, high and low. They were a major status symbol, and their manufacture and distribution were carefully controlled through a complicated institution known as the *ṭirāz*. Major events were at times celebrated by being depicted on silks. Many texts have been identified that describe the hundreds of different kinds of textiles that existed. Because textiles could easily be moved, they became a vehicle for the transmission of artistic themes within the Muslim world and beyond its frontiers. In the case of this one technique, therefore, one is dealing not simply with a medium of the decorative arts but with a key medium in the definition of a given time's taste, of its practical functions, and of the ways in which its ideas were distributed. The more unfortunate point is that the thousands of fragments that have remained have not yet been studied in a sufficiently systematic way, and in only a handful of instances has it been possible to relate individual fragments to known texts. When more work has been completed, however, a study of this one medium should contribute significantly to the commercial, social, and aesthetic history of Islam, as well as explain much of the impact that Islamic art had beyond the frontiers of the Muslim world.

The following survey of Islamic visual arts, therefore, will be primarily a historical one, for it is in development through time that the main achievements of Islamic art can best be understood. At the same time, other features peculiar to this tradition will be kept in mind: the varying importance of different lands, each of which had identifiable artistic features of its own, and the uniqueness of certain creative techniques.

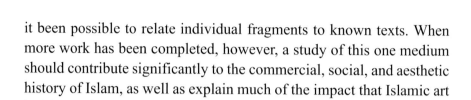

Chapter 1

Origins

Islamic visual arts were created by the confluence of a number of earlier artistic traditions and a new faith.

Earlier Artistic Traditions

The arts inherited by Islam were of extraordinary technical virtuosity and stylistic or iconographic variety. All the developments of arcuated and vaulted architecture that had taken place in Iran and in the Roman Empire were available in their countless local variants. Stone, baked brick, mud brick, and wood existed as mediums of construction, and all the complicated engineering systems developed particularly in the Roman Empire were still utilized from Spain to the Euphrates. All the major techniques of decoration were still used, except for monumental sculpture. In secular and in religious art, a more or less formally accepted equivalence between representation and represented subject had been established. Technically, therefore, as well as ideologically, the Muslim world took over an extremely sophisticated system of visual forms; and, because the Muslim conquest was accompanied by a minimum of destruction, all the monuments, and especially the attitudes attached to them, were passed on to the new culture.

The second point about the pre-Islamic traditions is the almost total absence of anything from Arabia itself. While archaeological work in the peninsula may modify this conclusion in part, it does seem that Islamic art formed itself entirely in some sort of relationship to non-Arab traditions. Even the rather sophisticated art created in earlier times by the Palmyrenes or by the Nabataeans had almost no impact on Islamic art, and the primitively conceived *ḥaram* in Mecca, the only pre-Islamic sanctuary maintained by the new faith, remained as a unique monument that was almost never copied or imitated despite its immense religious significance. The pre-Islamic sources of Islamic art are thus entirely extraneous to the milieu in which the new faith was created. In this respect the visual arts differ considerably from most other aspects of Islamic culture.

This is not to say that there was no impact of the new faith on the arts, but to a large extent it was an incidental impact, the result of the existence of a new social and political entity rather than of a doctrine. Earliest Islam as seen in the Qurʾān or in the more verifiable accounts of the Prophet's life simply do not deal with the arts, either on the practical level of requiring or suggesting forms as expressions of the culture or on the ideological level of defining a Muslim attitude toward images. In all instances, concrete Qurʾānic passages later used for the arts had their visual significance extrapolated.

There is no prohibition against representations of living things, and not a single Qurʾānic passage refers clearly to the mosque, eventually to become the most characteristically Muslim religious building. In the simple, practical, and puritanical milieu of early Islam, aesthetic or visual questions simply did not arise.

The Mosque

The impact of the faith on the arts occurred rather as the fledgling culture encountered the earlier non-Islamic world and sought to justify its own acceptance or rejection of new ways and attitudes. The discussion of two examples of particular significance illustrates the point. One is the case of the mosque. The word itself derives from the Arabic *masjid*, "a place where one prostrates oneself (in front of God)." It was a common term in pre-Islamic Arabic and in the Qur᾽ān, where it is applied to sanctuaries in general without restriction. If a more concrete significance was meant, the word was used in construct with some other term, as in *masjid al-ḥaram* to refer to the Meccan sanctuary. There was no need in earliest times for a uniquely Muslim building, for any place could be used for private prayer as long as the correct direction (*qiblah*, originally Jerusalem but very soon Mecca) was observed and the proper sequence of gestures and pious statements was followed. In addition to private prayer, which had no formal setting, Islam instituted a collective prayer on Fridays, where the same ritual was accompanied by a sermon from the imam (leader of prayer, originally the Prophet, then his successors, and later legally any able-bodied Muslim) and by the more complex ceremony of the *khuṭbah*, a collective swearing of allegiance to the community's leadership. This ceremony served to strengthen the common bond between all members of the *ummah*, the Muslim "collectivity," and its importance in creating and maintaining the unity of early Islam has often been emphasized. There were two traditional locales for this event in the Prophet's time. One was his private house, whose descriptions have been preserved; it was a large open space with private rooms on one side and rows of palm trunks making a colonnade on two other sides, the deeper colonnade being on the side of the qiblah. The Prophet's house was not a sanctuary but simply the most convenient place for the early community to gather. Far less is known about the second place of gathering for the Muslim community. It was used primarily on major feast days, such as the end of the fasting period or the feast of sacrifice. It was called a *muṣallā*, literally "a place for prayer," and muṣallās were usually located outside city walls. Nothing is known about the shape taken by muṣallās, but in all probability they were as simple as pre-Islamic pagan sanctuaries: large enclosures surrounded by a wall and devoid of any architectural or ornamental feature.

Altogether then there was hardly anything that could be identified as a holy building or as an architectural form. To be complete, one should add two additional features. One is an action, the call to prayer (*adhān*). It became, fairly rapidly, a formal moment preceding the gathering of the faithful. One man would climb on the roof and proclaim that God is great and that men must congregate to pray. There was no formal monument attached to the ceremony, though it led eventually to the ubiquitous minaret. The other early feature was an actual structure. It was the *minbar*, a chair with several steps on which the Prophet would climb in order to preach. The monument itself had a pre-Islamic origin, but Muhammad transformed it into a characteristically Muslim form.

With the exception of the minbar, only a series of actions were formulated in early Islamic times. There were no forms attached to them, nor were any needed. But, as the Muslim world grew in size, the contact with many other cultures brought about two developments. On the one hand, there were thousands of examples of beautiful religious buildings that impressed the conquering Arabs. But, more important, the need arose to preserve the restricted uniqueness of the community of faithful and to express its separateness from other groups. Islamic religious architecture began with this need and, in ways to be described later, created a formal setting for the activities, ceremonies, and ideas that had been formless at the outset.

The Prohibition Against Images

A second and closely parallel development of the impact of Islam on the visual arts is the celebrated question of a Muslim iconoclasm.

Tradition says Muhammad used a portable wooden minbar. In time the minbar became more permanent in nature, the number of steps increased, and it was commonly executed in stone or brick.

As has already been mentioned, the Qurʾān does not utter a word for or against the representation of living things. It is equally true that from about the middle of the 8th century a prohibition had been formally stated, and thenceforth it would be a standard feature of Islamic thought, even though the form in which it is expressed has varied from absolute to partial and even though it has never been totally followed. The justification for the prohibition tended to be that any representation of a living thing was an act of competition with God, for he alone can create something that is alive. It is striking that this theological explanation reflects the state of the arts in the Christian world at the time of the Muslim conquest—a period of iconoclastic controversy. It may thus be suggested that Islam developed an attitude toward images as it came into contact with other cultures and that its attitude was negative because the arts of the time appeared to lead easily to dreaded idolatry. While it is only by the middle of the 8th century that there is actual proof of the existence of a Muslim doctrine, it is likely that, more or less intuitively, the Muslims felt a certain reluctance toward representations from the very beginning. For all monuments of religious art are devoid of any representations; even a number of attempts at representational symbolism in the official art of coinage were soon abandoned.

This rapid crystallization of Islamic attitudes toward images has considerable significance. For practical purposes, representations are not found in religious art, although matters are quite different in secular art. Instead there occurred very soon a replacement of imagery with calligraphy and the concomitant transformation of calligraphy into a major artistic medium. Furthermore, the world of Islam tended to seek means of representing the holy other than by images of human beings, and one of the main problems of interpretation of Islamic art is that of the degree of means it achieved in this search. But there is a deeper aspect to this rejection of holy images. Although the generally

Semitic or specifically Jewish sources that have been given to Islamic iconoclasms have probably been exaggerated, the reluctance imposed by the circumstances of the 7th century transformed into a major key of artistic creativity the magical fear of visual imagery that exists in all cultures but that is usually relegated to a secondary level. This uniqueness is certainly one of the main causes of the abstract tendencies that are among the great glories of the tradition. Even when a major art of painting did develop, it remained always somehow secondary to the mainstream of the culture's development.

Both in the case of the religious building and in that of the representations, therefore, it was the contact with pre-Islamic cultures in Muslim-conquered areas that compelled Islam to transform its practical and unique needs into monuments and to seek within itself for intellectual and theological justifications for its own instincts. The great strength of early Islam was that it possessed within itself

The Dome of the Rock, in Jerusalem, is one of many works of Islamic architecture to employ calligraphy in its decorative scheme. The text used consists of passages from the Qurʾān.

ARABIC SCRIPT

Arabic is written from right to left and consists of 17 characters, which, with the addition of dots placed above or below certain of them, provide the 28 letters of the Arabic alphabet. Short vowels are not included in the alphabet, being indicated by signs placed above or below the consonant or long vowel that they follow. Certain characters may be joined to their neighbours, others to the preceding one only, and others to the succeeding one only. When coupled to another, the form of the character undergoes certain changes.

These features, as well as the fact that there are no capital forms of letters, give the Arabic script its particular character. A line of Arabic suggests an urgent progress of the characters from right to left. The balance between the vertical shafts above and the open curves below the middle register induces a sense of harmony. The peculiarity that certain letters cannot be joined to their neighbours provides articulation. For writing, the Arabic calligrapher employs a reed pen (*qalam*) with the working point cut on an angle. This feature produces a thick downstroke and a thin upstroke with an infinity of gradation in between. The line traced by a skilled calligrapher is a true marvel of fluidity and sensitive inflection, communicating the very action of the master's hand.

Broadly speaking, there were two distinct scripts in the early centuries of Islam: cursive script and Kūfic script. For everyday purposes a cursive script was employed: typical examples may be seen in the Arabic papyri from Egypt. Rapidly executed, the script does not appear to have been subject to formal and rigorous rules, and not all the surviving examples are the work of professional scribes. Kūfic script, however, seems to have been developed for religious and official purposes. The name means "the script of Kūfah," an Islamic city founded in Mesopotamia in 638 CE, but the actual connection between the city and the script is not clear. Kūfic is a rather square and angular script. Professional copyists employed a particular form for reproducing the earliest copies of the Qur'ān that have survived. These are written on parchment and date from the 8th to the 10th century. They are mostly of an oblong as opposed to codex (i.e., manuscript book) format. The writing is frequently large, especially in the early examples, so that there may be as few as three lines to a single page. The script can hardly be described as stiff and angular; rather, the implied pace is majestic and measured.

Kūfic went out of general use about the 11th century, although it continued to be used as a decorative element contrasting with those scripts that superseded it. About 1000 a new script was established and came to be used for copying the Qur'ān. This is the so-called *naskhī* script, which has remained perhaps the most popular script in the Arab world. It is a cursive script based on certain laws governing the proportions between the letters. The two names associated with its development are Ibn Muqlah and Ibn al-Bawwāb, both of whom lived and worked in Mesopotamia.

the ideological means to put together a visual expression of its own, even though it did not develop at the very beginning a need for such an expression.

One last point can be made about the origins of Islamic art. It concerns the degree of importance taken by the various artistic and cultural entities conquered by the Arabs in the 7th and 8th centuries, for the early empire had gathered in regions that had not been politically or even ideologically related for centuries. During the first century or two of Islam, the main models and the main sources of inspiration were certainly the Christian centres around the Mediterranean. But the failure to capture Constantinople (now Istanbul) and to destroy the Byzantine Empire also made those Christian centres inimical competitors, whereas the whole world of Iran became an integral part of the empire, even though the conquering Arabs were far less familiar with the latter than with the former. A much more complex problem is posed by conversions, for it is through the success of the militant Muslim religious mission that the culture expanded so rapidly. Insofar as one can judge, it is the common folk, primarily in cities, who took over the new faith most rapidly; and there thus was added in early Islamic culture a folk element whose impact may have been larger than has hitherto been imagined.

Those preliminary considerations on the origins of Islamic art have made it possible to outline several of the themes and problems that remained constant features of the tradition: a self-conscious sense of uniqueness when compared with others; a continuous reference to its own Qurʾānic sources; a constant relationship to many different cultures; a folk element; and a variety of regional developments. None of those features remained constant, not even those aspects of the faith that affected the arts. But while they changed, the fact of their existence, their structural presence, remained a constant of Islamic art.

CHAPTER 2

THE EARLY PERIOD

Of all the recognizable periods of Islamic art, this is by far the most difficult one to explain properly, even though it is quite well documented. There are two reasons for this difficulty. On the one hand, it was a formative period, a time when new forms were created that identify the aesthetic and practical ideals of the new culture. Such periods are difficult to define when, as in the case of Islam, there was no artistic need inherent to the culture itself. The second complication derives from the fact that Muslim conquest hardly ever destroyed a former civilization's established creativity. Material culture, therefore, continued as before, and archaeologically it is almost impossible to distinguish between pre-Islamic and early Islamic artifacts. Paradoxical though it may sound, there is an early Islamic Christian art of Syria and Egypt, and in many other regions the parallel existence of a Muslim and a non-Muslim art lasted for centuries. What did happen during early Islamic times, however, was the establishment of a dominant new taste, and it is the nature and character of this taste that has to be explained. It occurred first in Syria and Iraq, the two areas with the largest influx of Muslims and with the two successive capitals of the empire, Damascus under the Umayyads and Baghdad under the early ʿAbbāsids. From Syria and Iraq this new taste spread in all directions and adapted itself to local conditions and local materials, thus creating considerable regional and chronological variations in early Islamic art.

From a historical point of view, two major dynasties are involved. One is the Umayyad dynasty, which ruled from 661 to 750 and whose monuments are datable from 680 to 745. It was the only Muslim dynasty ever to control the whole of the Islamic-conquered world. The second dynasty is the ʿAbbāsid dynasty; technically its rule extended as late as 1258, but in reality its princes ceased to be a significant cultural factor after the second decade of the 10th century. The ʿAbbāsids no longer controlled Spain, where an independent Umayyad caliphate had been established; and in Egypt as well as in northeastern Iran a number of more or less independent dynasties appeared, such as the Ṭūlūnids or the Sāmānids. Although research in the late 20th century tends to make the conclusion less certain than it used to be for the Sāmānids and northeast Iran, the initial impulse for the artistic creativity of those dynasties came from the main ʿAbbāsid centres in Iraq. While in detailed studies it is possible to distinguish between Umayyad and ʿAbbāsid art or between the arts of various provinces, the key features of the first three centuries of Islamic art (roughly through the middle of the 10th century) are the interplay between local or imperial impulses and the creation of new forms and functions.

Architecture

It is possible to study the architecture of the Umayyad and ʿAbbāsid periods as a succession of clusters of monuments, but, because there are so many of them, a study can easily end up as an endless list. It is preferable, therefore, to centre the discussion of Umayyad and ʿAbbāsid monuments on the functional and morphological characteristics that identify the new Muslim world and only secondarily be concerned with stylistic progression or regional differences.

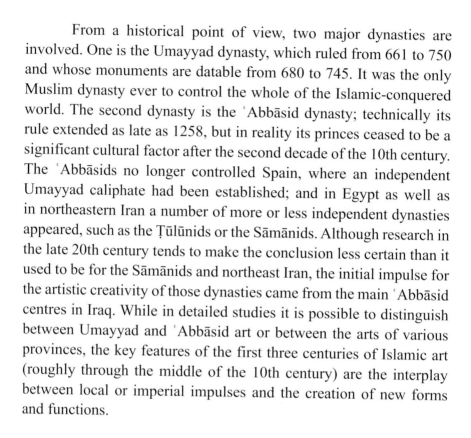

EARLY RELIGIOUS BUILDINGS

The one obviously new function developed during this period is that of the mosque, or *masjid*. The earliest adherents of Islam used the private house of the Prophet in Medina as the main place for their religious and other activities and muṣallās without established forms for certain holy ceremonies. The key phenomenon of the first decades that followed the conquest is the creation outside Arabia of *masjid*s in every centre taken over by the new faith. These were not simply or even primarily religious centres. They were rather the community centres of the faithful, in which all social, political, educational, and individual affairs were transacted. Among those activities were common prayer and the ceremony of the khuṭbah. The first mosques were built primarily to serve as the restricted space in which the new community would make its own collective decisions. It is there that the treasury of the community was kept, and early accounts are full of anecdotes about the immense variety of events, from the dramatic to the scabrous, that took place in mosques. Since even in earliest times the Muslim community consisted of several superimposed and interconnected social systems, mosques reflected this complexity, and, next to large mosques for the whole community, tribal mosques and mosques for various quarters of a town or city are also known.

None of those early mosques has survived, and no descriptions of the smaller ones have been preserved. There do remain, however, accurate textual descriptions of the large congregational buildings erected at Kūfah and Basra in Iraq and at Al-Fusṭāṭ in Egypt. At Kūfah a larger square was marked out by a ditch, and a covered colonnade known as a *ẓullah* (a shady place) was put up on the qiblah side. In 670 a wall pierced by many doors was built in place of the ditch, and colonnades were put up on all four sides, with a deeper one on the qiblah. In all probability the Basra mosque was very similar, and only minor differences distinguished the ʿAmr ibn al-ʿĀṣ mosque at Al-Fusṭāṭ. Much has been written about the sources of this type of building, but the simplest explanation may be that this is the very rare instance of the actual creation of a new architectural type. The new faith's requirement for centralization, or a space for a large and constantly growing community, could not be met by any existing architectural form. Almost accidentally, therefore, the new Muslim cities of Iraq created the hypostyle mosque (a building with the roof resting on rows of columns). A flexible architectural unit, a hypostyle structure could be square or rectangular and could be increased or diminished in size by the addition or subtraction of columns. The single religious or symbolic feature of the hypostyle mosque was a minbar for the preacher, and the direction of prayer was indicated by the greater depth of the colonnade on one side of the structure.

The examples of Kūfah, Basra, and Al-Fusṭāṭ are particularly clear because they were all built in newly created cities. Matters are somewhat more complex when discussing the older urban centres taken over by Muslims. Although it is not possible to generalize with any degree of certainty, two patterns seem to emerge. In some cases, such as Jerusalem and Damascus and perhaps in most cities conquered through formal treaties, the Muslims took for themselves an available unused space and erected on it some shelter, usually a very primitive one. In Jerusalem this space happened to be a particularly holy one—the area of the Jewish temple built by Herod the Great, which had been left willfully abandoned and ruined by the triumphant Christian empire. In Damascus it was a section of a huge Roman temple area, on another part of which there was a church. Unfortunately, too little is known about other cities to be able to demonstrate that this pattern was a common one. The very same uncertainty surrounds the second pattern, which consisted in forcibly transforming sanctuaries of older faiths into Muslim ones. This was the case at Ḥamāh in Syria and at Yazd-e Khvāst in Iran, where archaeological proof exists of the change. There are also several literary references to the fact that Christian churches, Zoroastrian fire temples, and other older abandoned sanctuaries were transformed into mosques. Altogether, however, those instances probably were not too numerous, because in most places the Muslim conquerors were quite eager to preserve local tradition and because few older sanctuaries could easily serve the primary Muslim need of a large centralizing space.

During the 50 years that followed the beginning of the Muslim conquest, the mosque, until then a very general concept in Islamic thought, became a definite building reserved for a variety of needs required by the community of faithful in any one settlement. Only in one area, Iraq, did the mosque acquire a unique form of its own, the oriented hypostyle. Neither in Iraq nor elsewhere is there evidence of symbolic or functional components in mosque design. The only exception is that of the *maqṣūrah* (literally "closed-off space"), an enclosure, probably in wood, built near the centre of the qiblah wall. Its purpose was to protect the caliph or his replacement, for several attacks against major political figures had taken place. But the maqṣūrah was never destined to be a constant fixture of mosques, and its typological significance is limited.

THREE GREAT MOSQUES

During the rule of the Umayyad prince al-Walīd I (705–715), a number of complex developments within the Muslim community were crystallized in the construction of three major mosques—at Medina, Jerusalem, and Damascus. The very choice of those three cities is indicative: the city in which the Muslim state was formed and in which the Prophet was buried; the city held in common holiness by Jews, Christians, and Muslims, which was rapidly accruing the mystical hagiography surrounding the Prophet's ascension into heaven; and the ancient city that became the capital of the new Islamic empire. A first and essential component of al-Walīd's mosques was thus their imperial character; they were to symbolize the permanent establishment of the new faith and of the state that derived from it. They were no longer purely practical shelters but willful monuments.

Although the plans of Al-Aqṣā Mosque in Jerusalem and of the mosque of Medina can be reconstructed with a fair degree of certainty, only the one at Damascus has been preserved with comparatively minor alterations and repairs. In plan the three buildings appear at first glance to be quite different from each other. The Medina mosque was essentially a large hypostyle with a courtyard. The colonnades on all four sides were of varying depth. Al-Aqṣā Mosque consisted of an undetermined number of naves (possibly as many as 15) parallel to each other in a north-south direction. There was no courtyard, because the rest of the huge esplanade of the former Jewish temple served as the open space in front of the building. The Umayyad Mosque of Damascus is a rectangle 515 by 330 feet (157 by 100 metres) whose outer limits and three gates are parts of a Roman temple (a fourth Roman gate on the qiblah side was blocked). The interior consists of an open space surrounded on three sides by a portico and of a covered space of three equal long naves parallel to the qiblah wall that are cut in the middle by a perpendicular nave.

The three buildings share several important characteristics. They are all large spaces with a multiplicity of internal supports, and although only the Medina mosque is a pure hypostyle, the Jerusalem and Damascus mosques have the flexibility and easy internal communication characteristic of a hypostyle building. All three mosques exhibit a number of distinctive new practical elements and symbolic

The Umayyad Mosque is also known as the Great Mosque of Damascus. It stands on the site of a 1st-century Hellenic temple to Jupiter and of a later church of St. John the Baptist.

meanings. Many of those occur in all mosques; others are known in only some of them. The *mihrab*, for example, appears in all mosques. This is a niche of varying size that tends to be heavily decorated. It occurs in the qiblah wall, and, in all probability, its purpose was to commemorate the symbolic presence of the Prophet as the first imam, although there are other explanations. It is in Damascus only that the ancient towers of the Roman building were first used as minarets to call the faithful to prayer and to indicate from afar the presence of Islam (initially minarets tended to exist only in predominantly non-Muslim cities). All three mosques are also possed an axial nave, a wider aisle unit on the axis of the building, which served both as a formal axis for compositional purposes and as a ceremonial one for the prince's retinue. Finally, all three buildings were heavily decorated with marble, mosaics, and woodwork. At least in the mosque of Damascus, it is further apparent that there was careful concern for the formal composition—a balance between parts that truly makes this mosque a work of art. This is particularly evident in the successful relationship established between the open space of the court and the facade of the covered qiblah side.

When compared with the first Muslim buildings of Iraq and Egypt, the monuments of al-Walīd are characterized by the growing complexity of their forms, by the appearance of uniquely Muslim symbolic and functional features, and by the quality of their construction. While the dimensions, external appearance, and proportions of any one of them were affected in each case by unique local circumstances, the internal balance between open and covered areas and the multiplicity of simple and flexible supports indicate the permanence of the early hypostyle tradition.

Other Classic Mosques

Either in its simplest form, as in Medina, or in its more-formalized shape, as in Damascus, the hypostyle tradition dominated mosque architecture from 715 to the 10th century. As it occurs at Nīshāpūr (Neyshābūr) in northeastern Iran, Sīrāf in southern Iran, Kairouan in Tunisia, and Córdoba in Spain, it can indeed be considered as the classic early Islamic type. Its masterpieces occur in Iraq and in the West. The monumentalization of the early Iraqi hypostyle is illustrated by the two ruined structures in Sāmarrāʾ, with their enormous sizes (790 by 510 feet [240 by 156 metres] for one and 700 by 440 feet [213 by 135 metres] for the other), their multiple entrances, their complex piers, and, in one instance, a striking separation of the qiblah area from the rest of the building. The best-preserved example of this type is the Mosque of Aḥmad ibn Ṭūlūn at Cairo (876–879), where a semi-independent governor, Aḥmad ibn Ṭūlūn, introduced Iraqi techniques and succeeded in creating a masterpiece of composition.

Two classic examples of early mosques in the western Islamic world are preserved in Tunisia and Spain. In Kairouan the Great Mosque was built in stages between 836 and 866. Its most striking feature is the formal emphasis on the building's T-like axis punctuated by two domes, one of which hovers over the earliest preserved ensemble of mihrab, minbar, and maqṣūrah. At Córdoba the earliest section of the Great Mosque was built in 785–786. It consisted simply of 11 naves with a wider central one and a court. It was enlarged twice in length, first between 833 and 855 and again from 961 to 965 (it was in the latter phase that the celebrated maqṣūrah and mihrab, composing one of the great architectural ensembles of early Islamic art, were constructed). Finally, in 987–988 an extension of the mosque was completed to the east that increased its size by almost one-third without destroying its stylistic unity. The constant increases in the size of this mosque are a further illustration of the flexibility of the hypostyle and its adaptability to any spatial requirement. The most memorable aspects of the Córdoba

The dome of the mirab of the Great Mosque of Córdoba is made from a single block of marble. Carved in the form of a shell, its walls are inlaid with Byzantine-style mosaics and gold.

DOME OF THE ROCK

The Dome of the Rock, in Jerusalem, is a unique building. Completed in 691, this masterwork of Islamic architecture is the earliest major Islamic monument. Its octagonal plan, use of a high dome, and building techniques are hardly original, although its decoration is unique. Its purpose, however, is what is most remarkable about the building.

Since the middle of the 8th century, the Dome of the Rock has become the focal centre of the most mystical event in the life of the Prophet: his ascension into heaven from the rock around which the building was erected. According to an inscription preserved since the erection of the dome, however, it would seem that the building did not originally commemorate the Prophet's ascension but rather the Christology of Islam and its relationship to Judaism. It seems preferable, therefore, to interpret the Dome of the Rock as a victory monument of the new faith's ideological and religious claim on a holy city and on all the religious traditions attached to it.

mosque, however, lie in its construction and decoration. The particularly extensive and heavily decorated mihrab area exemplifies a development that started with the Medina mosque and would continue: an emphasis on the qiblah wall.

Although the hypostyle mosque was the dominant plan, it was not the only one. From very early Islamic times, a fairly large number of other plans also occur. Most of them were built in smaller urban locations or were secondary mosques in larger Muslim cities. It is rather difficult, therefore, to evaluate whether their significance was purely local or they were important for the tradition as a whole. Because a simple type of square subdivided by four piers into nine-domed units occurs at Balkh in Afghanistan, at Cairo, and at Toledo, it may be considered a pan-Islamic type. Other types, a single square hall surrounded by an ambulatory, or a single long barrel-vault parallel or perpendicular to the qiblah, are rarer and should perhaps be considered as purely local. These are particularly numerous in Iran, where it does seem that the mainstream of early Islamic architecture did not penetrate very deeply. Unfortunately, the archaeological exploration of Iran is still in its infancy, and many of the mud-brick buildings from the early Islamic period have been destroyed or rebuilt beyond recognition. As a result, it is extremely difficult to determine the historical importance of monuments found at Neyrīz, Moḥammadīyeh (near Nāʾīn), Fahraj (near Yazd), or Hazareh (near Samarkand). For an understanding of the mosque's development and of the general dynamics of Islamic architecture, however, an awareness of those secondary types, which may have existed outside Iran as well, is essential.

Other Types of Religious Buildings

The function of the mosque, the central gathering place of the Muslim community, became the major and most original completely Muslim architectural effort. The mosque was not a purely religious building, at least not at the beginning, but, because it was restricted to Muslims, it is appropriate to consider it as such. This, however, was not the only type of early Islamic building to be uniquely Muslim.

One little-known, if distinctly Islamic, type of religious building is the *ribāṭ*. As early as in the 8th century, the Muslim empire entrusted the protection of its frontiers, especially the remote ones, to warriors for the faith (*murābiṭūn*, "bound ones") who lived, permanently or temporarily, in special institutions known as ribāṭs. Evidence for these exist in Central Asia, Anatolia, and North Africa. It is only in Tunisia that ribāṭs

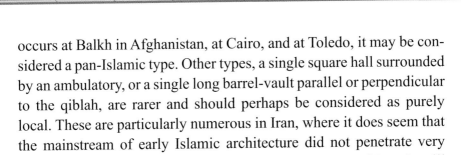

The ribāṭ at Sousse was built in the 9th century. A ribāṭ was basically a fortified monastery, serving both religious and military functions.

have been preserved. The best one is at Sousse, Tunisia; it consists of a square fortified building with a single fairly elaborate entrance and a central courtyard. It has two stories of private or communal rooms. Except for the prominence taken by an oratory, this building could be classified as a type of Muslim secular architecture. Because no later example of a ribāṭ is known, there is some uncertainty as to whether the institution ever acquired a unique architectural form of its own.

The last type of religious building to develop before the end of the 10th century is the mausoleum. Originally, Islam was strongly opposed to any formal commemoration of the dead. But three independent factors slowly modified an attitude that was eventually maintained only in the most strictly orthodox circles. One factor was the growth of the Shīʿite heterodoxy, which led to an actual cult of the descendants of the Prophet through his son-in-law ʿAlī. The second factor was that, as Islam strengthened its hold on conquered lands, a wide variety of local cultic practices and especially the worship of certain sacred places began to affect the Muslims, resulting in a whole movement of Islamization of ancient holy places by associating them with deceased Muslim heroes and holy men or with prophets. The third factor is not, strictly speaking, religious, but it played a major part. As more or less independent local dynasties began to grow, they sought to commemorate themselves through mausoleums. Not many mausoleums have remained from those early centuries, but literary evidence is clear on the fact that the Shīʿite sanctuaries of Karbalāʾ and Al-Najaf, both in Iraq, and Qom, Iran, already possessed monumental tombs. At Sāmarrāʾ an octagonal mausoleum had been built for three caliphs. The masterpieces of early funerary architecture occur in Central Asia, such as the royal mausoleum of the Sāmānids (known incorrectly as the mausoleum of Esmāʿīl the Sāmānid) at Bukhara (before 942), which is a superb example of Islamic brickwork. In some instances a quasi-religious character was attached to the mausoleums, such as the one at Tim (976), which already has the high facade typical of so many later monumental tombs. In all instances the Muslims took over or rediscovered the ancient tradition of the centrally planned building as the characteristic commemorative structure.

The royal mausoleum of the Sāmānids is in Bukhara, which was the capital of the Sāmānid dynasty in the 9th and 10th centuries. It is the only fully preserved monument that remains from the Sāmānid capital.

The other important kind of Muslim religious building to develop during this period is the *madrasah*, an institution for religious training set up independently of mosques. It is known from texts that such privately endowed schools existed in the northeastern Iranian world as early as the 9th century, but no description exists of how they looked or were planned.

Secular Architecture

Whereas the functions of the religious buildings of early Islam could not have existed without the new faith, the functions of secular Muslim architecture have a priori no specifically Islamic character. This is all the more so since one can hardly point to a significant new need or habit that would have been brought from Arabia by the conquering Muslims and because so little was destroyed in the conquered areas. It can be assumed, therefore, that all pre-Islamic functions such as living, trading, and manufacturing continued in whatever architectural setting they may have had. Only one exception is certain. With the disappearance of Sāsānian kingship, the pre-Islamic Iranian imperial tradition ceased, and elsewhere conquered minor kings and governors left their palaces and castles. A new imperial power was created, located first in Damascus, then briefly in the northern Syrian town of Al-Ruṣāfah, and eventually in Baghdad and Sāmarrā᾽ in Iraq. New governors and, later, almost independent princes took over provincial capitals, which sometimes were old seats of government and at other times were new Muslim centres. In all instances, however, there is no reason to assume that for an architecture of power or of pleasure early Muslims would have felt the need to modify pre-Islamic traditions. In fact, there is much in early Islamic secular architecture that can be used to illustrate secular arts elsewhere—in Byzantium, for example, or even in the

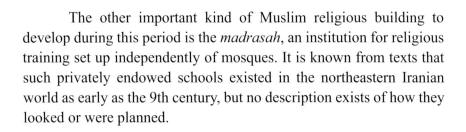

West. If any new political or social entity is to succeed in preserving an identity of its own, however, it must give to its secular needs certain directions and emphases that will eventually establish a unique cultural image. This is what happened in the development of Umayyad and early ʿAbbāsid secular architecture.

Three factors contributed to the evolution of a new secular architecture. One was that the accumulation of an immense wealth of ideas, workers, and money in the hands of the Muslim princes settled in Syria and Iraq gave rise to a unique palace architecture. The second factor was the impetus given to urban life and to trade. New cities were founded from Sijilmassa on the edge of the Moroccan Sahara to Nīshāpūr in northeastern Iran, and 9th-century Arab merchants traded as far away as China. Thus, the second topic, to be treated below, will be the urban design and commercial architecture. The third factor is that, for the first time since Alexander the Great, a world extending from the Mediterranean to India became culturally unified. As a result, decorative motifs, design ideas, structural techniques, and artisans and architects—which until then had belonged to entirely different cultural traditions—were available in the same places. Early Islamic princely architecture has become the best-known and most original aspect of early Islamic secular buildings.

There are basically three kinds of these princely structures. The first type consists of 10 large rural princely complexes found in Syria, Palestine, and Transjordan dating from about 710 to 750: Al-Ruṣāfah, Qaṣr al-Ḥayr East, Qaṣr al-Ḥayr West, Khirbat Minyah, Jabal Says, Khirbat al-Mafjar, Mshattā, Qaṣr ʿAmrah, Qaṣr al-Kharānah, and Qaṣr al-Ṭūbah. Apparently, those examples of princely architecture belong to a group of more than 60 ruined or only textually identifiable rural complexes erected by Umayyad princes. In the past a romantic theory had developed about their locations, suggesting that the remoteness of their sites expressed an atavistic hankering on the part of the

This floor panel mosaic depicting gazelles and a lion is from the 8th-century Khirbat al-Mafjar complex, north of Jericho in the West Bank. This Umayyad desert palace is also known as Hishām's Palace.

Umayyad Arab rulers for the desert or at least the semiarid steppe that separates the permanently cultivated areas of Syria and Palestine from their original home in the north Arabian wilderness. This theory has been disproved, for every one of those has turned out to have been a major agricultural or trade centre, some of which were developed even before the Muslim conquest. Private palaces were built, notably those at Al-Ruṣāfah, Qaṣr al-Ḥayr West, Khirbat al-Mafjar, Qaṣr ʿAmrah, and Mshattā. Those must be considered as early medieval equivalents of the *villae rusticae* so characteristic in the ancient Roman period. Although each of those had a number of idiosyncrasies that were presumably inspired by the needs and desires of its owner, all those structures tend to share a number of features that can best be illustrated by Khirbat al-Mafjar.

That palace, the richest of them all, contained a residential unit consisting of a square building with an elaborate entrance, a porticoed courtyard, and a number of rooms or halls arranged on two floors. Few of those rooms seem to have any identifiable function, although at Khirbat al-Mafjar a private oratory, a large meeting hall, and an anteroom leading to a cool underground pool have been identified. The main throne room was on the second floor above the entrance. Its plan is not known but probably resembled the preserved throne rooms or reception halls at Qaṣr ʿAmrah and Mshattā, which consisted of a three-aisled hall ending in an apse (semicircular or polygonal domed projection) in the manner of a Roman basilica.

Next to an official residence, there usually was a small mosque, generally a miniaturized hypostyle in plan. The most original feature of those establishments was the bath. The bathing area itself is comparatively small, but every bath had its own elaborate entrance and contained a large hall that, at least in the instance of Khirbat al-Mafjar, was heavily decorated and of an unusual shape. It would appear that those halls were for pleasure—places for music and dancing. In some instances, as at Qaṣr ʿAmrah, the same setting may have been used for both pleasure and formal receptions.

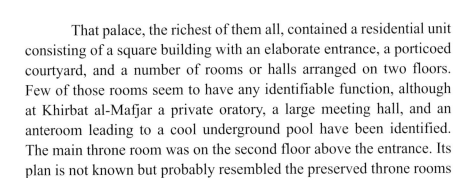

Those palaces are important illustrations of the luxurious taste and way of life of the new Middle Eastern aristocrats, who settled in the countryside and transformed some of it into places of pleasure. This aspect of those establishments is peculiar to the Umayyad dynasty in Syria and Palestine. Outside this area and period only one comparable structure has been found—at Ukhayḍir in Iraq, which dates from the early ʿAbbāsid period. A number of princely residences of the Central Asian or North African countryside are still too little known but appear not to have had the same development. The other important lesson to draw from them is that few of their features are original. All of them derive from the architectural vocabulary of pre-Islamic times, and it is in the artistic traditions of the Mediterranean world that most of their sources are found, although the Mshattā throne room does have a number of Sāsānian elements. For this reason, those palaces should be considered major examples of pre-Islamic secular architecture, for as interesting as they are, these monuments are not part of the Islamic tradition.

A second type of princely architecture—the urban palace—has been preserved only in texts or literary sources, with the exception of the palace at Kūfah in Iraq. Datable from the very end of the 7th century, this example of princely architecture seems to have functioned both as a residence and as the *dār al-imārah*, or centre of government. This dual function is reflected in the use of separate building units and in the absence of much architectural decoration, which suggests that it reflected an austere official taste. Although suggestions concerning the plans used are occasionally encountered in literary sources, this information is not sufficient to define those early urban official buildings of the Muslims. Nothing is known, for instance, about the great Umayyad palace in Damascus aside from the fact that it had a green dome.

Also poorly documented is a development in urban aristocratic buildings that seems to have begun with the ʿAbbāsids during the last decades of the 8th century. This involved the construction of smaller palaces, probably pavilions in the midst of gardens in or around major cities.

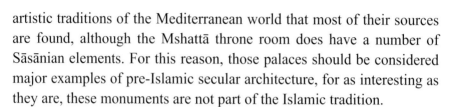

The palace-city is the third type of early Islamic princely architecture. Several of these huge palaces are part of the enormous mass of ruins at Sāmarrāʾ, the temporary ʿAbbāsid capital from 838 to 883. Jawsaq al-Khāqānī, for instance, is a walled architectural complex nearly one mile to a side that in reality is an entire city. It contains a formal succession of large gates and courts leading to a cross-shaped throne room, a group of smaller living units, basins and fountains, and even a racetrack. Too little is known about the architectural details of those huge walled complexes to lead to more than very uncertain hypotheses. Their existence, however, suggests that they were settings for the very elaborate ceremonies developed by the ʿAbbāsid princes, especially when receiving foreign ambassadors. An account, for instance, in Khaṭīb al-Baghdādī's (died 1071) *Ta'rīkh Baghdad* ("History of Baghdad") of the arrival in Baghdad of a Byzantine envoy in 914 illustrates this point. The meeting with the caliph was preceded by a sort of formal presentation intended to impress the ambassador with the Muslim ruler's wealth and power. Treasures were laid down; thousands of soldiers and slaves in rich clothes guarded them; lions roared in the gardens; and on gilded artificial trees mechanical devices made silver birds chirp. The ceremony was a fascinating mixture of a traditional attempt to re-create paradise on earth and a rather vulgar exhibition of wealth that required a huge space, as in the Sāmarrāʾ palaces. Another important aspect of those palace-cities is that they became part of a myth. The walled enclosure in which thousands lived a life unknown to others and into which simple mortals did not penetrate without bringing their own shroud was transformed into legend. It became the mysterious City of Brass of *The Thousand and One Nights*, and it is from its luxurious glory that occasionally a caliph such as Hārūn al-Rashīd escaped into the "real" world. Even information on the ʿAbbāsid palace-city is inadequate; it was clearly a unique early Islamic creation, and its impact can be detected from Byzantium to Hollywood.

Urban Design

Islamic secular architecture has left considerable information about cities, for systematic urbanization was one of the most characteristic features of early Muslim civilization. It is much too early to draw any sort of conclusion about the actual physical organization of towns, about their subdivisions and their houses, for only at Al-Fusṭāṭ (Cairo) and Sīrāf in Iran is the evidence archaeologically clear, and much of it has not yet been properly published. A huge task remains to relate the immense amount of textual material with scraps of archaeological information scattered from Central Asia to Spain. In general, it can be said that there does not seem to have been any idealized master plan for the internal arrangement of an urban site, in contradistinction to Hellenistic or Roman towns. Even mosques or palaces were often located eccentrically and not in the middle of the town. Extraordinary attention was paid to water distribution and conservation, as demonstrated by the magnificent 9th-century cisterns in Tunisia, the 9th-century Nilometer (a device to measure the Nile's level) in Cairo, and the elaborate dams, canals, and sluices of Qaṣr al-Ḥayr in Syria. The construction of commercial buildings on a monumental scale occurred. The most spectacular example is the caravansary of Qaṣr al-Ḥayr East, with its magnificent gate.

The concern for palaces and cities that characterized early Islamic secular architecture shows itself most remarkably in the construction of Baghdad between 762 and 766–767 by the ʿAbbāsid caliph al-Manṣūr. It was a walled round city whose circular shape served to demonstrate Baghdad's symbolic identity as the navel of the universe. A thick ring of residential quarters was separated by four axial commercial streets entered through spectacular gates. In the centre of the city there was a large open space with a palace, a mosque, and a few administrative buildings. By its size and number of inhabitants, Baghdad was unquestionably a city; however, its plan so strongly emphasized the presence of the caliph that it was also a palace.

Building Materials and Technology

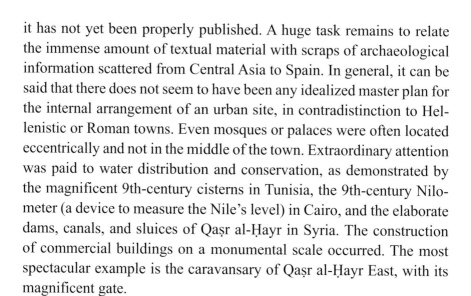

The early Islamic period, on the whole, did not innovate much in the realm of building materials and technology, but utilized what it had inherited from older traditions. Stone and brick continued to be used throughout the Mediterranean, whereas mud brick usually covered with plaster predominated in Iraq and Iran, with a few notable exceptions such as Sīrāf, where a masonry of roughly cut stones set in mortar was more common. The most important novelty was the rapid development in Iraq of a baked brick architecture in the late 8th and 9th centuries. Iraqi techniques were later used in Syria at Al-Raqqah and Qaṣr al-Ḥayr East and in Egypt. Iranian brickwork appears at Mshattā in Jordan. The mausoleum of the Sāmānids in Bukhara is the earliest remaining example of the new brick architecture in northeastern Iran. Wood was used consistently but usually has not been very well preserved, except in Palestine and Egypt, where climatic (extreme dryness of Egypt), religious (holiness of Jerusalem sanctuaries), or historic (Egypt was never conquered) factors contributed to the continuous upkeep of wooden objects and architectural elements.

As supports for roofs and ceilings, early Islamic architecture used walls and single supports. Walls were generally continuous, often buttressed with half towers, and rarely (with exceptions in Central Asia) were they articulated or broken by other architectural features. The most common single support was the base-column-capital combination of Mediterranean architecture. Most columns and capitals either were reused from pre-Islamic buildings or were directly imitated from older models. In the 9th century in Iraq a brick pier was used, a form that spread to Iran and Egypt. Columns and piers were covered with arches. Most often these were semicircular arches; the pointed, or two-centred, arch was known, but it does not seem that its property of reducing the need for heavy supports had been realized. The most extraordinary technical development of arches occurs in the Great Mosque at Córdoba, where, in order to increase the height of the building in an area with only short columns, the architects created two rows of superimposed horseshoe arches. Almost immediately they realized that such a succession of superimposed arches constructed of alternating stone and brick could be modified to create a variety of patterns that would alleviate the inherent monotony of a hypostyle building. A certain ambiguity remains, however, as to whether ornamental effect or structural technology was the predominate concern in the creation of those unique arched columns.

The majority of early Islamic ceilings were flat. Gabled wooden roofs, however, were erected in the Muslim world west of the Euphrates and simple barrel vaults to the east. Vaulting, either in brick or in stone, was used, especially in secular architecture. Domes were employed frequently in mosques, consistently in mausoleums, and occasionally in secular buildings. Almost all domes are on squinches (supports carried across corners to act as structural transitions to a dome). Most squinches, as in the Kairouan domes, are classical Greco-Roman

The Great Mosque of Córdoba's 850 pillars divide its interior into 19 north-to-south and 29 east-to-west aisles, with each row of pillars supporting a tier of open horseshoe arches upon which a third and similar tier is superimposed.

niches, which transform the square room into an octagonal opening for the dome. In Córdoba's Great Mosque a complex system of intersecting ribs is encountered, whereas at Bukhara the squinch is broken into halves by a transverse half arch. The most extraordinary use of the squinch occurs in the mausoleum at Tim, where the surface of this structural device is broken into a series of smaller three-dimensional units rearranged into a sort of pyramidal pattern. This rearrangement is the earliest extant example of *muqarnas*, or stalactite-like decoration that would later be an important element of Islamic architectural ornamentation. The motif is so awkwardly constructed at Tim that it must have derived from some other source, possibly the ornamental device of using curved stucco panels to cover the corners and upper parts of walls found in Iran at Nīshāpūr.

Architectural Decoration

Early Islamic architecture is most original in its decoration. Mosaics and wall paintings followed the practices of antiquity and were primarily employed in Syria, Palestine, and Spain. Stone sculpture existed, but stucco sculpture, first limited to Iran, spread rapidly throughout the early Islamic world. Not only were stone or brick walls covered with large panels of stucco sculpture, but this technique was used for sculpture in the round in the Umayyad palaces of Qaṣr al-Ḥayr West and Khirbat al-Mafjar. The latter was a comparatively short-lived technique, although it produced some of the few instances of monumental sculpture anywhere in the early Middle Ages. A variety of techniques borrowed from the industrial arts were used for architectural ornamentation. The mihrab wall of Kairouan's Great Mosque, for example, was covered with ceramics, whereas fragments of decorative woodwork have been preserved in Jerusalem and Egypt.

The themes and motifs of early Islamic decoration can be divided into three major groups. The first kind of ornamentation simply emphasizes the shape or contour of an architectural unit. The themes used were vegetal bands for vertical or horizontal elements, marble imitations for the lower parts of long walls, chevrons or other types of borders on floors and domes, and even whole trees on the spandrels or soffits (undersides) of arches as in the Umayyad Mosque of Damascus or the Dome of the Rock; all these motifs tend to be quite traditional, being taken from the rich decorative vocabularies of pre-Islamic Iran or of the ancient Mediterranean world.

The second group consists of decorative motifs for which a concrete iconographic meaning can be given. In the Dome of the Rock and the Umayyad Mosque of Damascus, as well as possibly the mosques of Córdoba and of Medina, there were probably iconographic programs. It has been shown, for example, that the huge architectural and vegetal decorative motifs at Damascus were meant to symbolize a sort of idealized paradise on earth, whereas the crowns of the Jerusalem sanctuary are thought to have been symbols of empires conquered by Islam. But it is equally certain that this use of visual forms in mosques for ideological and symbolic purposes was not easily accepted, and most later mosques are devoid of iconographically significant themes. The only exceptions fully visible are the Qurʾānic inscriptions in the mosque of Ibn Ṭūlūn at Cairo, which were used both as a reminder of the faith and as an ornamental device to emphasize the structural lines of the building. Thus, the early Islamic mosque eventually became austere in its use of symbolic ornamentation, with the exception of the mihrab, which was considered as a symbol of the unity of all believers.

Like religious architecture, secular buildings seem to have been less richly decorated at the end of the early Islamic period than at the beginning. The paintings, sculptures, and mosaics of Qaṣr al-Ḥayr West, Khirbat al-Mafjar, Qaṣr ʿAmrah, and Sāmarrāʾ primarily illustrated

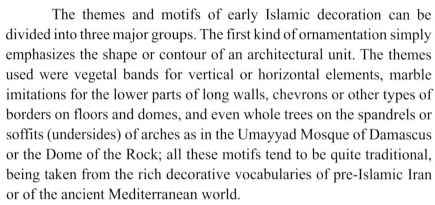

The Dome of the Rock's structure and ornamentation are rooted in the Byzantine architectural tradition, yet it represents an early stage in the emergence of a distinct Islamic visual style.

the life of the prince. There were official iconographic compositions, such as the monarch enthroned, or ones of pleasure and luxury, such as hunting scenes or depictions of the prince surrounded by dancers, musicians, acrobats, and unclad women. Few of these so-called princely themes were iconographic inventions of the Muslims. They usually can be traced back either to the classical world of ancient Greece and Rome or to pre-Islamic Iran and Central Asia.

The third type of architectural decoration consists of large panels, most often in stucco, for which no meaning or interpretation is yet known. Those panels might be called ornamental in the sense that their only apparent purpose was to beautify the buildings in which they were installed, and their relationship to the architecture is arbitrary. The Mshattā facade's decoration of a huge band of triangles is, for instance, quite independent of the building's architectural parts. Next to Mshattā, the most important series of examples of the third type of ornamentation come from Sāmarrāʾ, although striking examples are also to be found at Khirbat al-Mafjar, Qaṣr al-Ḥayr East and West, Al-Fusṭāṭ, Sīrāf, and Nīshāpūr. Two decorative motifs were predominately used on those panels: a great variety of vegetal motifs and geometric forms. At Sāmarrāʾ those panels eventually became so abstract that individual parts could no longer be distinguished, and the decorative design had to be viewed in terms of the relationships between line and shape, light and shade, horizontal and vertical axes, and so forth. Copied consistently from Morocco to Central Asia, the aesthetic principles of this latter type of a complex overall design influenced the development of the principle of arabesque ornamentation.

Islamic architectural ornamentation does not lend itself easily to chronological stylistic definition. In other words, it does not seem to share consistently a cluster of formal characteristics. The reason is that in the earliest Islamic buildings the decorative motifs were borrowed from an extraordinary variety of stylistic sources: classical themes that were illusionistically rendered (e.g., the mosaics of the Umayyad Mosque of Damascus), hieratic Byzantine themes (e.g., the Umayyad Mosque of Damascus and Qaṣr ʿAmrah), Sāsānian motifs, Central Asian motifs (especially the sculpture from Umayyad palaces), and the many regional styles of ornamentation that had developed in all parts of the pre-Islamic world. It is the wealth of themes and motifs, therefore, that constitutes the Umayyad style of architectural decoration. The ʿAbbāsids, on the other hand, began to be more selective in their choice of ornamentation.

The walls of the Umayyad Mosque were once covered with more than an acre (450 square kilometers) of mosaics depicting a fanciful landscape thought to be the Qurʾānic paradise, but only fragments survive.

Decorative Arts

The most important medium of early Islamic decorative arts is pottery. Initially Muslims continued to sponsor whatever varieties of ceramics had existed before their arrival. Probably in the last quarter of the 8th century, new and more elaborate types of glazed pottery were produced. This new development did not replace the older and simpler types of pottery but added a new dimension to the art of Islamic ceramics. Because of the still incompletely published studies on the unfinished excavations carried out at Nīshāpūr, Sīrāf, Qaṣr al-Ḥayr

East, and Al-Fusṭāṭ, the scholarship on those ceramics is likely to be very much modified. Therefore, this section will treat only the most general characteristics of Islamic ceramics, avoiding in particular the complex archaeological problems posed by the growth and spread of individual techniques.

The area of initial technical innovation seems to have been Iraq. Trade with Central Asia brought Chinese ceramics to Mesopotamia, and Islamic ceramicists sought to imitate them. It is probably in Iraq, therefore, that the technique of lustre glazing was first developed in the Muslim world. This gave the surface of a clay object a metallic, shiny appearance. Egypt also played a leading part in the creation of the new ceramics. Because the earliest datable lustre object (a glass goblet with the name of the governor who ruled in 773, now in the Cairo Museum of Islamic Ceramics) was Egyptian, some scholars feel that it was in Egypt and not Iraq that lustre was first used. Early pottery was also produced in northeastern Iran, where excavations at Afrāsiyāb (Samarkand) and Nīshāpūr have brought to light a new art of painted underglaze pottery. Its novelty was not so much in the technique of painting designs on the slip and covering them with a transparent glaze as in the variety of subjects employed.

While new ceramic techniques may have been sought to imitate other mediums (mostly metal) or other styles of pottery (mostly Chinese), the decorative devices rapidly became purely and unmistakably Islamic in style. A wide variety of motifs were combined: vegetal arabesques or single flowers and trees; inscriptions, usually legible and consisting of proverbs or of good wishes; animals that were usually birds drawn from the vast folkloric past of the Middle East; occasionally human figures drawn in a strikingly abstract fashion; geometric designs; all-over abstract patterns; single motifs on empty fields; and simple splashes of colour, with or without underglaze sgraffito designs (i.e., designs incised or sketched on the body or the slip of the object). All these motifs were

Samarkand ware has backgrounds of black, red, and creamy white with decorations in green, yellow, pink, and brown. The most famous, and perhaps oldest, examples have Kūfic lettering inscribed in black on white ground.

used on both the high-quality ceramics of Nīshāpūr and Samarkand as well as on Islamic folk pottery.

Although ceramics appear to be the most characteristic medium of expression in the decorative arts during the early Islamic period, it is only because of the greater number of preserved objects. Glass was as important, but examples have been less well preserved. A tradition of ivory carving developed in Spain, and the objects dating from the last third of the 10th century onward attest to the high quality of this uniquely Iberian art. Many of those carved ivories certainly were made for princes; therefore, it is not surprising that their decorative themes were drawn from the whole vocabulary of princely art known through Umayyad painting and sculpture of the early 8th century. Those ivory carvings are also important in that they exemplify the fact that an art of sculpture in the round never totally disappeared in the Muslim world—at least in small objects.

Very little is known about early Islamic gold and silver objects, although their existence is mentioned in many texts as well as suggested by the wealth of the Muslim princes. Except for a large number of silver plates and ewers belonging to the Sāsānian tradition, nothing has remained. Those silver objects were probably made for Umayyad and ʿAbbāsid princes, although there remains much controversy among scholars regarding both their authenticity and the date of their manufacture.

For entirely different reasons it is impossible to present any significant generalities about the art of textiles in the early Islamic period. Problems of authenticity are few, however. Dating from the 10th century are a large number of Būyid silks, a group of funerary textiles with plant and animal motifs as well as poetic texts. Very little order has yet been made of an enormous mass of often well-dated textile fragments, and, therefore, except for the Būyid silks, it is still impossible to identify any one of the textile types mentioned in early medieval literary sources. Furthermore, because it can be safely assumed that the pre-Islamic textile factories were taken over by the Muslims and because it is otherwise known that textiles were easily transported from one area of the Muslim world to the other or even beyond it, it is still very difficult to define Islamic styles as opposed to Byzantine or to Coptic ones. The obvious exception lies in those fragments that are provided with inscriptions, and the main point to make is, therefore, that one of the characteristic features of early Islamic textiles is their use of writing for identifying and decorative purposes. But, while true, this point in no way makes it possible to deny an Islamic origin to fragments that are not provided with inscriptions, and one must thus await further investigations of detail before being able to assign defining characteristics to early Islamic textiles.

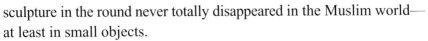

ASSESSMENT

There are three general points that seem to characterize the art of the early Islamic period. It can first be said that it was an art that sought self-consciously, like the culture sponsoring it, to create artistic forms that would be identifiable as being different from those produced in preceding or contemporary non-Islamic artistic traditions. At times, as in the use of the Greco-Roman technique of mosaics or in the adoption of Persian and Roman architectural building technology, early Islamic art simply took over whatever traditions were available. At other times, as in the development of the mosque as a building type, it recomposed into new shapes the forms that had existed before. On the other hand, in ceramics or the use of calligraphic ornamentation, the early Islamic artists invented new techniques and a new decorative vocabulary. Whatever the nature of the phenomenon, it was almost always an attempt to identify itself visually as unique and different. Because there was initially no concept about what should constitute an Islamic tradition in the visual arts, the early art of the Muslims often looks like only a continuation of earlier artistic styles, forms, subjects, and techniques. Many mosaics, silver plates, or textiles, therefore, were not considered Islamic until recently. In order, then, to understand them as examples of the art of a new culture, those early buildings and objects have to be seen in the complete context in which they were created. When so seen, they appear as conscious choices by the new Islamic culture from its immense artistic inheritance.

A second point of definition concerns the question of whether there is an early Islamic style or perhaps even several styles in some sort of succession. The fascinating fact is that there is a clear succession only in those artistic features that are Islamic inventions—nonfigurative ornament and ceramics. For it is only in development of those features that one can find the conscious search for form that can create a period style. Elsewhere, especially in palace art, the Muslim world sought to relate itself to an earlier and more universal tradition of princely art; its monuments, therefore, are less Islamic than typological. In the new art of the Muslim bourgeoisie, however, uniquely Islamic artistic phenomena began to evolve.

Finally, the geographical peculiarities of early Islamic art must be reiterated. Its centres were Syria, Iraq, Egypt, northwestern Iran, and Spain. Of these, Iraq was probably the most originally creative, and it is from Iraq that a peculiarly Islamic visual koine (a commonly accepted and understood system of forms) was derived and spread throughout the Islamic world. This development, of course, is logical, because the capital of the early empire and some of the first purely Muslim cities were in Iraq. In western Iran, in Afghanistan, in northern Mesopotamia, and in Morocco, the more atypical and local artistic traditions were more or less affected by the centralized imperial system of Iraq. This tension between a general pan-Islamic vocabulary and a variable number of local vocabularies was to remain a constant throughout the history of Islamic art and is certainly one of the reasons for the difficulty, if not impossibility, one faces in trying to define an Islamic style.

CHAPTER 3

MIDDLE PERIOD

The middle period in the development of Islamic art extends roughly from the year 1000 to 1500, when a strong central power with occasional regional political independence was replaced by a bewildering mosaic of overlapping dynasties. Ethnically, this was the time of major Turkish and Mongol invasions that brought into the Muslim world new peoples and institutions. At the same time, Imazighen (Berbers), Kurds, and Iranians, who had been within the empire from the beginning of Islam, began to play far more effective historical and cultural roles, short-lived for the Kurds but uniquely important for the Iranians. Besides political and ethnic confusion, there was also religious and cultural confusion during the middle period. The 10th century, for example, witnessed the transformation of the Shīʿite heterodoxy into a major political and possibly cultural phenomenon, while the extraordinary development taken by the personal and social mysticism known as Sufism modified enormously the nature of Muslim piety. Culturally, the most significant development was perhaps that of Persian literature as a highly original new verbal expression existing alongside the older Arabic literary tradition. Finally, the middle period was an era of geopolitical expansion in all areas except Spain, which the Muslims completely lost in 1492 with the conquest of the kingdom of Granada by Ferdinand II and Isabella. Anatolia and the Balkans, the Crimean Peninsula, much of Central Asia and northern India, and parts of eastern Africa all became new Islamic provinces. In some cases this expansion was the result of conquests, but in others it had been achieved through missionary work.

The immense variety of impulses that affected the Muslim world during those five centuries was one of the causes of the bewildering artistic explosion that also characterizes the middle period.

Fāṭimid Art (909–1171)

The Fāṭimids were technically an Arab dynasty professing with missionary zeal the beliefs of the Ismāʿīlī sect of the Shīʿite branch of Islam. The dynasty was established in Tunisia and Sicily in 909. In 969 the Fāṭimids moved to Egypt and founded the city of Cairo. They soon controlled Syria and Palestine. In the latter part of the 11th century, however, the Fāṭimid empire began to disintegrate internally and externally; the final demise occurred in 1171. But it is not known which of the obvious components of the Fāṭimid world was more significant in influencing the development of the visual arts: its heterodoxy, its Egyptian location, its missionary relationship with almost all provinces of Islam, or the fact that during its heyday in the 11th century it was the only wealthy Islamic centre and could thus easily gather artisans and art objects from all over the world.

Architecture

The great Fāṭimid mosques of Cairo—Al-Azhar (started in 970) and Al-Ḥākim (*c.* 1002–03)—were designed in the traditional hypostyle plan with axial cupolas. It is only in such architectural details as the elaborately composed facade of Al-Ḥākim, with its corner towers and vaulted portal, that innovations appear, for most earlier mosques did not have large formal gates, nor was much attention previously given to the composition of the exterior facade. Fāṭimid architectural traditionalism was certainly a conscious attempt to perpetuate the existing aesthetic system.

Although much less is known about it, the Great Palace of the Fāṭimids belonged to the tradition of the enormous palace-cities typical of the ʿAbbāsids. Mediterranean rather than Iranian influences, however, played a greater part in the determination of its uses and functions. The whole city of Cairo (Arabic: *Al-Qāhirah*, "The Victorious"), on the other hand, has many symbolic and visual aspects that suggest a willful relationship to Baghdad.

The originality of Fāṭimid architecture does not lie in the works sponsored by the caliphs themselves, even though Cairo's well-preserved gates and walls of the second half of the 11th century are among the best examples of early medieval military architecture. It is rather the patronage of lower officials and of the bourgeoisie, if not even of the humbler classes, that was responsible for the most interesting Fāṭimid buildings. The mosques of Al-Aqmar (1125) and of Al-Ṣāliḥ (*c.* 1160) are among the first examples of monumental small mosques constructed to serve local needs. Even though their internal arrangement is quite traditional, their plans were adapted to the space available in the urban centre. These mosques were elaborately decorated on the exterior, exhibiting a conspicuousness absent from large hypostyle mosques.

A second innovation in Fāṭimid architecture was the tremendous development of mausoleums. This may be explained partially by Shīʿism's emphasis on the succession of holy men, but the development of these buildings in terms of both quality and quantity indicates that other influential social and religious issues were also involved.

The Al-Aqmar Mosque, in Cairo, is also known as the Grey Mosque. Its intricately carved facade runs parallel to the street, but the qiblah orientation of the hypostyle mosque is still maintained.

Most of the mausoleums were simple square buildings surmounted by a dome. Many of these have survived in Cairo and Aswān. Only a few, such as the *mashhad* at Aswān, are somewhat more elaborate, with side rooms. The most original of these commemorative buildings is the Juyūshī Mosque (1085) overlooking the city of Cairo. Properly speaking, it is not a mausoleum but a monument celebrating the reestablishment of Fāṭimid order after a series of popular revolts.

The Fāṭimids introduced, or developed, only two major constructional techniques: the systematization of the four-centred keel arch and the squinch. The latter innovation is of greater consequence because the squinch became the most common means of passing from a square to a dome, although pendentives were known as well. A peculiarly Egyptian development was the muqarnas squinch, which consisted of four units: a niche bracketed by two niche segments, superimposed with an additional niche. The complex profile of the muqarnas became an architectural element in itself used for windows, while the device of using niches and niche segments remained typical of Egyptian decorative design for centuries. It still is impossible to say whether the muqarnas was invented in Egypt or inspired by other architectural traditions (most likely Iranian). Fāṭimid domes were smooth or ribbed and developed a characteristic "keel" profile.

In the use of materials (brick, stone, wood) and structural concepts, Fāṭimid architecture continued earlier traditions. Occasionally, local styles were incorporated, among them features of Tunisian architecture in the 10th century or of upper Mesopotamian in the late 11th century.

Stone sculpture, stuccowork, and carved wood were utilized for architectural decorations. The Fāṭimids also employed mosaicists, who mostly worked in places like Jerusalem, where they imitated or repaired earlier mosaic murals. Many fragments of Fāṭimid wall paintings have survived in Egypt. Most of them, however, are too small to allow for making any iconographic or stylistic conclusions, with the exception of the mid-12th-century ceiling of the Palatine Chapel at Palermo. Built by the Norman kings of Sicily, the palace chapel was almost certainly decorated by Fāṭimid artists, or at least the artists adhered to Fāṭimid models. The hundreds of facets in the muqarnas ceiling were painted, notably with many purely ornamental vegetal and zoomorphic designs but also with scenes of daily life and many subjects that have not yet been explained. Stylistically influenced by Iraqi ʿAbbāsid art, these paintings are innovative in their more spatially aware representation of personages and of animals. Very similar tendencies appear also in the stucco and wood sculptures of Fāṭimid decoration. The stunning abstraction of the architectural decoration at Sāmarrāʾ tends to give way to more naturalistically conceived vegetal and animal designs; occasionally, whole narrative scenes appear carved on wood. Another decorative trend is especially used on 12th-century mihrabs: explicitly complicated geometric patterns, usually based on stars, which in turn generate octagons, hexagons, triangles, and rectangles. Geometry becomes a sort of network containing small vegetal units, often as inlaid pieces. Long inscriptions written in very elaborate calligraphies also became a typical form of architectural decoration on most of the major Fāṭimid buildings.

Decorative Arts

A clear separation must be made between the decorative arts sought by Fāṭimid princes and the arts produced within their empire. Little has been preserved of the former, notably a small number of superb ewers in rock crystal. A text has survived, however, that describes the imperial treasures looted in the middle of the 11th century by dissatisfied mercenary troops. It lists gold, silver, enamel, and porcelain objects that have all been lost, as well as textiles (perhaps the cape of the Norman king

FĀṬIMID BOOK ILLUSTRATION

Manifestations of nonprincely Fāṭimid art also included the art of book illustration. The few remaining fragments illustrate that probably after the middle of the 11th century there developed an art of representation other than the style used to illustrate princely themes. This was a more illusionistic style that still accompanied the traditional ornamental one in the same manner as in the paintings on ceramics.

In summary it would appear that Fāṭimid art was a curiously transitional one. Although much influenced by earlier Islamic and non-Islamic Mediterranean styles, the Fāṭimids devised new structural systems and developed a new manner of painting representational subjects, which became characteristic of all Muslim art during the 12th century. Neither documentary nor theoretical research in Islamic art, however, has developed sufficiently to clearly establish whether the Fāṭimids were indeed innovators or whether their art was a local phenomenon that is only accidentally relatable to what followed.

Roger II is an example of the kind of textiles found in this treasure). The inventory also records that the Fāṭimids had in their possession many works of Byzantine, Chinese, and even Greco-Roman provenance. Altogether, then, it seems that the imperial art of the Fāṭimids was part of a sort of international royal taste that downplayed cultural or political differences.

Ceramics, on the other hand, were primarily produced by local urban schools and were not an imperial art. The most-celebrated type of Fāṭimid wares was lustre-painted ceramics from Egypt itself. A large number of artisans' names have been preserved, thereby indicating the growing prestige of these craftsmen and the aesthetic importance of their pottery. Most of the surviving lustre ceramics are plates on which the decoration of the main surface has been emphasized. The decorative themes used were quite varied and included all the traditional Islamic ones—e.g., calligraphy, vegetal and animal motifs, arabesques. The most-distinguishing feature of these Fāṭimid ceramics, however, is the representation of the human figure. Some of these ceramics have been decorated with simplified copies of illustrations of the princely themes, but others have depictions of scenes of Egyptian daily life. The style in which these themes have been represented is simultaneously the hieratic, ornamental manner traditional to Islamic painting combined with

This lusterware plate with a decoration of a gazelle on it was made in Egypt during the Fāṭimid period. The Fāṭimid period is arguably the high point for Islamic pottery in Egypt.

what can almost be called spatial illusionism. Wheel-cut rock crystal, glass, and bronze objects, especially animal-shaped aquamaniles (a type of water vessel) and ewers, are also attributed to the Fāṭimids.

Seljuq Art

During the last decades of the 10th century, at the Central Asian frontiers of Islam, a migratory movement of Turkic peoples began that was to affect the whole Muslim world up to and including Egypt. The dominant political force among those Turks was the dynasty of the Seljuqs, but it was not the only one; nor can it be demonstrated, as far as the arts are concerned, that it was the major source of patronage in the period to be discussed anywhere but in Anatolia in the 12th and 13th centuries. The Seljuq empire, therefore, consisted of a succession of dynasties, and all but one (the Ayyūbids of Syria, Egypt, and northern Mesopotamia) were Turkic.

A complex feudal system was established and centred on urban areas. Cities were established or expanded, particularly in western Iran, Anatolia, and Syria. Militant Muslims, the Seljuqs also sought to revive Muslim orthodoxy. Although politically unruly and complicated in their relationships to one another, the successive and partly overlapping dynasties of the Ghaznavids, Ghūrids, Great Seljuqs (Turkmens of the Iranian plateau), Qarakhānids, Zangids, Ayyūbids, Seljuqs of Rūm, and Khwārezm-Shahs (considering only the major ones) seem to have created a comparatively unified culture from India to Egypt. The art of the Seljuq period, however, is difficult to discuss coherently, both because of the wealth of examples and because of the lack of synchronization between various technical and regional developments. This complex world fell apart under the impact of the Mongol invasions that, from 1220 until 1260, swept through the Muslim lands of the Middle East.

Characteristic Architectural Forms

The functions of monumental architecture in the Seljuq period were considerably modified. Large congregational mosques were still built. The earliest Seljuq examples occur in the two major new provinces of Islam—Anatolia and northwestern India—as well as in the established Muslim region of western Iran. In some areas, such as the Eṣfahān region, congregational mosques were rebuilt, while in other parts of the Islamic world, such as Syria or Egypt, where there was no need for new large mosques, older ones were repaired and small ones were built. The latter were partly restricted to certain quarters or groups or were commissioned by various guilds, particularly in Damascus.

A curious side aspect of the program of building, rebuilding, or decorating mosques was the extraordinary development of minarets. Particularly in Iran, dozens of minarets are preserved from the 12th and 13th centuries, while the mosques to which they had been attached have disappeared. It is as though the visual function of the minaret was more important than the religious institution to which it was attached.

Small or large, mausoleums increased in numbers and became at this time the ubiquitous monument they appear to be. Most of the mausoleums, such as the tomb tower of Abū Yazīd al-Bisṭāmī (died 874) at Basṭām, were dedicated to holy men—both contemporary Muslim saints and all sorts of holy men dead for centuries (even pre-Islamic holy men, especially biblical prophets, acquired a monument). The most impressive mausoleums, however, like the one of Sanjarat Merv, were built for royalty. Pilgrimages were organized and in many places hardly mentioned until then as holy places (e.g., Mashhad, Basṭām, Mosul, Aleppo); a whole monastic establishment serving as a centre for the distribution of alms was erected with hostels and kitchens for the pilgrims.

Although enormously expanded, mosques, minarets, and mausoleums were not new types of Islamic architecture. The madrasah (school), however, was a new building type. There is much controversy as to why and how it really developed. Although early examples have been discovered in Iran, such as the 11th-century madrasah of Khargird, and at Samarkand (now in Uzbekistan), it is from Anatolia, Syria, and Egypt that most of the information about the madrasah has been derived. In the latter regions it was usually a privately endowed establishment reserved for one or two of the schools of jurisprudence of orthodox Islam. It had to have rooms for teaching and living quarters for the students and professors. Often the tomb of the founder was attached to the madrasah. Later madrasahs were built for two or three schools of jurisprudence, and the Mustanṣiriyyah in Baghdad was erected in 1233 to be a sort of ecumenical madrasah for the whole of Sunni Islam.

During the Seljuq period there occured a revival of the hostel-like ribāṭ inside cities. *Khānqāh*s (monastic complexes), monasteries, and various establishments of learning other than formal madrasahs were also built.

An impressive development of secular architecture occurred under the Seljuqs. The most characteristic building of the time was the citadel, or urban fortress, through which the new princes controlled the usually alien city they held in fief. The largest citadels, like those of Cairo and Aleppo, were whole cities with palaces, mosques, sanctuaries, and baths. Others, like the citadel of Damascus, were simpler constructions. Occasionally, as in the Euphrates valley, single castles were built, possibly in imitation of those constructed by the Christian Crusaders. Walls surrounded most cities, and all of them were built or rebuilt during the Seljuq period.

Little is known about Seljuq palaces or private residences in general. A few fragments in Konya or in Mosul are insufficient to give a coherent idea about urban palaces, and it is only in Anatolia and in

CARAVANSARIES

The caravansary (also spelled caravanserai) is a public building used for sheltering caravans and other travelers found throughout the Middle East and in parts of North Africa and Central Asia. The caravansary is usually constructed outside the walls of a town or village. The structure is quadrangular in form and is enclosed by a massive wall that has small windows near the top and only a few narrow air holes near the bottom. A heavy-doored gateway, high and wide enough to admit loaded camels, is usually the sole entrance; it can be secured from within by massive iron chains, which are drawn across it at night. Their gates are often decorated with intricate carving, as is the prayer niche within.

Inside, the ground floor consists of a central court surrounded by a cloisterlike arcade, which is in turn surrounded by cellular storerooms. The ground floor is connected by broad, open, stone stairways to a second story that is ringed by a somewhat lighter arcade, which gives access to many small rooms. The ground floor is used for storing the bales of merchandise or stabling the camels, and meals are cooked in the corner of the quadrangle; upstairs rooms are for lodging. The central court is paved with flagstones and is usually large enough to contain 300 or 400 crouching camels or tethered mules. The court is open to the sky and has a well with a fountain basin in its centre.

Neither food nor provender are supplied in a caravansary, but a porter appointed by the municipal authority is always present, lodged just within the gate. He and his assistants guard the building and the goods and persons within it and have the right to maintain order there. The caravansary is always kept open for all arrivals from early dawn until late in the evening.

Khans are often confused with caravansaries, but these places are analogous to inns and hotels, where not only lodging but food and other comforts may be had for payment. Khans are generally located within the town or village precincts, provide more elaborate lodgings, and are much smaller than caravansaries.

Central Asia that an adequate idea of other types can be obtained. Anatolian palaces are on the whole rather small villa-like establishments, but, in Afghanistan and Central Asia, excavations at Tirmidh, Lashkarī Bāzār, and Ghaznī have brought to light a whole group of large royal palaces erected in the 11th and early 12th centuries.

Commercial architecture became very important. Individual princes and cities probably were trying to attract business by erecting elaborate caravansaries on the main trade routes, such as Ribāṭ-i Malik, built between Samarkand and Bukhara in Uzbekistan. The most spectacular caravansaries were built in the 13th century in Anatolia. Equally impressive, however, although less numerous, are the caravansaries erected in eastern Iran and northern Iraq. Bridges also were rebuilt and decorated like the one at Cizre in Turkey.

The forms of architecture developed by the Seljuqs were remarkably numerous and varied considerably from region to region. Because the Iranian innovations dating from the 11th century and first half of the 12th century are the earliest and, therefore, probably influenced all other areas of the Seljuq empire, they will be discussed first.

Architecture in Iran

Even though it is not entirely typical, the justly celebrated Great Mosque of Eṣfahān was one of the most influential of all early Seljuq religious structures. Probably completed about 1130 after a long and complicated history of rebuildings, it consisted of a large courtyard onto which opened four large vaulted halls known as *eyvāns*; the eyvāns created the compositional axes of each side of the court. On the side of the qiblah (which indicates the direction of the sacred shrine of the Kaʿbah, faced by the faithful during prayers), the hall of the main eyvān was followed by a huge cupola. The area between eyvāns was subdivided into a large number of square bays covered by domes. The Eṣfahān mosque also had a unique feature: on the north side a single domed hall positioned on the main axis of the building was in all probability a formal hall for princes to change their clothes before entering into the sanctuary of the mosque.

The two features of the Great Mosque at Eṣfahān that became characteristic of Seljuq mosques were the eyvān and the dome. The eyvān was an architectural element known already in Sāsānian architecture that had been used in residential buildings from Egypt to Central Asia before the 11th century. In fact, the use of the *eyvān* was not restricted to just mosques; it also appears in palaces (Lashkarī Bāzār), caravansaries (Rebāṭ-e Sharaf), and madrasahs. The eyvān was, in other words, a unit of architectural composition that had no specific use and, therefore, no meaning. In the mosques of the 12th century, four eyvāns were used, at least in the clearly definable architectural school of western Iran (e.g., Ardestān, Zavāreh). This kind of composition had two principal effects. One was that the eyvāns centralized the visual effect of the mosque by making the courtyard the centre of the building. The other effect of this composition was that it broke up into four areas what had for centuries been a characteristic of the mosque: its single, unified space. The reasons for those developments are still speculative.

Whether large or small, cupolas or domes were used in mosques, caravansaries, and palaces. They were the main architectural features of almost all mausoleums, where they were set over circular

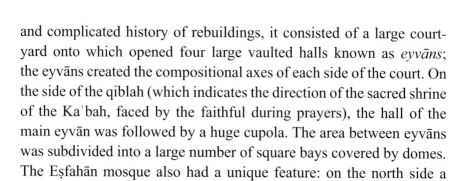

The Great Mosque at Eṣfahān is also known as the Masjed-e Jāmeʿ, or "Universal Mosque." The complex, framed by four huge *eyvāns*, includes structures built from the 11th century to the 18th—among them, private chapels, a school, a library, and a treasury.

or polygonal rooms.

Domes and eyvāns indicate that the central concern of Iranian construction during the Seljuq period was vaulting in baked brick, which became the main vehicle for any monumental construction (mud brick was used for secondary parts of a building, frequently for certain secular structures). A large and forcefully composed octagonal base developed the muqarnas squinch from a purely ornamental feature into one wherein both structural and decorative functions combined. In some later buildings, such as the mausoleum of Sanjarat Merv, a system of ribs was used to vault an octagonal zone. Seljuq architects sought to make their domes visible from afar and for that reason invented the double dome. Its outer shell was raised on a high drum, while the interior kept the traditional sequence: square base, zone

Standing alone in a desolate region, the minaret of Jām escaped discovery until 1957. It is conjectured that the minaret may mark the position of the lost Ghūrid capital of Fīlūzkūh.

of transition, and dome. Using this structural device, therefore, exterior height was achieved without making the exterior dome too heavy and without complicating the task of decorating the interior, always a problem in countries like Iran with limited supplies of wood for scaffolding. Domes along the eyvāns were another factor that contributed to the growing separation between the exterior and the interior view of a building. The construction of tall circular or polygonal minarets and high facades also indicate an emphasis on visibility from a distance.

Two characteristic Iranian architectural forms are not present in the Great Mosque of Eṣfahān but occur elsewhere in the city. One is the tower. Those narrow and tall (up to about 150 feet [50 metres]) were minarets, of which several dozen have been preserved all over Iran and Central Asia (such as the one at Jām). Shorter and squatter towers were mausoleums. Those were particularly typical of northern Iran. The other characteristic architectural type exists only in Eṣfahān in a much-damaged state. It is the *pīshṭāq*, a formal gateway that served to emphasize a building's presence and importance.

Architectural decoration was intimately tied to structure. Two mediums predominated. One was stucco, which continued to be used to cover large wall surfaces. The other was brick. Originating in the 10th-century architecture of northeastern Iran, brick came to be employed as a medium of construction as well as a medium of decoration. The complex decorative designs worked out in brick often had a rigidly geometric effect. Especially cut shapes of terra-cotta and brick, frequently produced in unusual sizes, served to soften those geometric patterns by modifying their tactile impact and by introducing additional curved or beveled lines to the straight lines of geometry.

Paintings were used for architectural decoration, especially in palaces. From the second half of the 12th century, coloured tiles began to be utilized to emphasize the contour of a decorative area in a structural unit; tiles were not used to cover whole walls, however. There are also examples of architectural sculpture of animals and people.

Most of the decorative designs tended to be subordinated to geometry, and even calligraphic or vegetal patterns were affected by a seemingly mathematically controlled aesthetic. It has been suggested that those complex geometric designs were a result of an almost mystical passion for number theories that were popularized in 11th-century Iran by such persons as the scholar and scientist al-Bīrūnī or the poet-mathematician Omar Khayyam. But even if the impulses for geometric design were originally created at the highest intellectual level, the designs themselves rapidly became automatic patterns. Their quality was generally high, but a tendency toward facility can be observed in such buildings as Rebāṭ-e Sharaf.

Architecture in Iraq, Syria, and Anatolia

In Iraq, northern Mesopotamia, Syria, and Egypt (after 1171) the architectural monuments do not, on the whole, appear to be as overwhelmingly impressive as those of Iran, largely because the taste of Umayyad and ʿAbbāsid times continued to dominate mosque architecture. It is in the construction of new building types, particularly the madrasah, that the most originality is apparent. The Syrian madrasahs in Damascus, like Al-ʿĀdiliyyah, Al-Ẓāhiriyyah, or the works of Nureddin, tended also to follow a comparatively standardized plan: an elaborate facade led into a domed hallway and then into a court with at least one eyvān. Most of those madrasahs were small and were fitted into a preexisting urban pattern. The use of eyvāns and the construction of the many minarets found in Mosul or on the Euphrates certainly attest to the influence of Iranian Seljuq design.

The main achievement of Ayyūbid, Zangid, or Seljuq architecture in the Fertile Crescent was the translating into stone of new structural systems first developed in brick. The most impressive instance of this lies in the technically complex muqarnas domes and half domes or in the muqarnas pendentives of Syrian buildings. Elaborate mihrabs were also made of multicoloured stones that were carefully cut to create impressive patterns. The architecture of the Fertile Crescent, therefore, was still dominated by the sheer force of stone as a material for both construction and decoration, and, therefore, the architecture was more Mediterranean in effect than were the buildings of Iran.

This Mediterranean tendency was evident in the 13th-century architecture of Seljuq Anatolia as well. This new province of Islam was rapidly populated with new immigrants and consequently gathered themes and motifs from throughout the Muslim world, as well as from the several native Anatolian traditions of Byzantine, Armenian, and Georgian architecture. The resulting assimilation of styles produced an overwhelmingly original architecture, for each building in Konya, Kayseri, Sivas, Divriği, and Erzurum and on the roads between them is a unique monument.

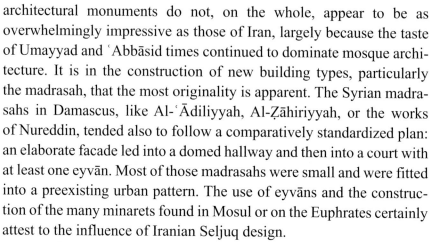

Functionally, the buildings in Anatolia do not differ from those in other parts of the Muslim world. All the structural forms found in Syria and Iran can be found in Anatolia as well, although they have often been adapted to local materials. Three uniquely Anatolian architectural features, however, can be distinguished. One was limited to Konya at this time but would have an important widespread development later on. As it appears in the Ince or Karatay *medrese*s (madrasahs), it consists of the transformation of the central courtyard into a domed space while maintaining the eyvān. Thus, the centralized aspect of the eyvān plan becomes architecturally explicit. The second feature is the creation of a facade that usually consisted of a high central portal—often framed by two minarets—with an elaborately sculpted decorative composition that extended to two corner towers. The third distinguishing feature of Anatolian Seljuq architecture is the complexity of the types of funerary monuments that were constructed.

From the point of view of construction, most of Anatolian architecture is of stone. In Konya and a number of eastern Anatolian instances, brick was used. Barrel vaults, groin vaults, muqarnas vaults, squinch domes, pendentive domes, and the new pendentive known as Turkish triangle (a transformation of the curved space of the traditional pendentive into a fanlike set of long and narrow triangles built at an angle from each other) were all used by Anatolian builders, thereby initiating the great development of vault construction in Ottoman architecture.

Architectural decoration consisted primarily in the stone sculpture found on the facades of religious and secular buildings. Although influenced by Iran and Syria in many details, most Anatolian themes were original, although some exhibit Armenian and possibly Western influences. The exuberance of Anatolian architectural decoration can perhaps be best demonstrated in the facades of Sivas's Gök Medrese and of Konya's Ince Minare. In addition to the traditional geometric,

This view of Ince Minare, in Konya, Turkey, shows the sculptural ornamentation of the main facade portal and the decorative brickwork of the minaret. The former *medrese* is now a museum.

epigraphic, and vegetal motifs, a decorative sculpture in the round or in high relief was created that included many representations of human figures and especially animals. Whether this sculpture is essentially a reflection of the decorative wealth of pre-Islamic monuments in Anatolia or whether it is a vestige of a pagan Turkish art that originated in Central Asia is still an unsolved historical problem.

There are few examples of wall painting from Anatolia. Especially in Konya, however, a major art of painted-tile decoration did evolve, possibly developed by Iranian artists who fled from the Mongol onslaught.

In summing up the architectural development of the Seljuq period, three points seem to be particularly significant. One is the expansion of building typology and the erection of new monumental architectural forms, thus illustrating an expansion of patronage and a growing complexity of taste. The second point is that, regardless of the quality and interest of monuments in the Fertile Crescent, Egypt, and Anatolia, the most inventive and exciting architecture in the 11th and 12th centuries was that of Iran. But, far more than in the preceding period, regional needs and regional characteristics seem to predominate over synchronic and pan-Islamic ones. Finally, there was a striking growth of architectural decoration both in sophistication of design and in variation of technique.

Other Arts

Although probably not as varied as architecture, the other arts of the Seljuq period also underwent tremendous changes. They demonstrate an extraordinary artistic energy, a widening of the social patronage of the arts, and a hitherto unknown variety of topics and modes of expression. It was as though the Seljuq period was gathering a sort of aesthetic momentum, but that effort seems to have been curtailed by the Mongol invasion. Chronologically, almost all surviving documentation and examples of those arts date from the latter part of the period, after 1150. It is unclear whether this apparent date is merely an accidental result of what has been preserved and is known through later scholarship or whether it corresponds to some precise event or series of events.

Glass and textiles continued to be major mediums during the Seljuq period. Ceramics underwent many changes, especially in Iran, where lustre painting became widespread and where new techniques were developed for colouring pottery. Furthermore, the growth of tile decoration created a new dimension for the art of ceramics.

Inlaid metalwork became an important technique. First produced at Herāt in Iran (now in Afghanistan) in the middle of the 12th century, this type of decoration spread westward, and a series of local schools were established in various regions of the Seljuq domain. In this technique the surfaces of utilitarian metallic objects (candlesticks, ewers, basins, kettles, and so forth) were engraved, and then silver was inlaid in the cut-out areas to make the decorative design more clearly visible.

Manuscript illustration also became an important art. Scientific books, including the medical manuals of Pedanius Dioscorides and of Galen, or literary texts such as the picaresque adventures of a

This leaf from the *Maqāmāt* of al-Hariri shows camels with their driver. The illustration is the work of Yahya ibn Mahmud al-Wasiti, of the Baghdad school, and is now in the Bibliothèque Nationale, in Paris.

verbal genius known as the *Maqāmāt*, were produced with narrative illustrations throughout the text.

All the technical novelties of the Seljuqs seem to have had one main purpose: to animate objects and books and to provide them with clearly visible and identifiable images. Even the austere art of calligraphy became occasionally animated with letters ending in human figures. The main centres for producing these arts were located in Iran and the Fertile Crescent. For reasons yet unknown, Egypt and Anatolia were far less involved. One reason may be that those two Seljuq provinces did not witness the same rise of an urban middle class as did Iran, Iraq, and Syria. It would seem from a large number of art objects whose patrons are known that the main market for these works of art was the mercantile bourgeoisie of the big cities and not, as has often been believed, the princes. Seljuq decorative arts and book illustration, therefore, reflect an urban taste.

The themes and motifs used were particularly numerous. In books they tend to be illustrations of the text, even if a manuscript such as the so-called Schefer *Maqāmāt* (1237; named for the French

Orientalist and bibliophile Charles-Henri-Auguste Schefer [1820–98], who once owned it) sought to combine a strict narrative with a fairly naturalistic panorama of contemporary life. Narrative scenes taken from books or reflecting folk stories are also common on Persian ceramics. In all mediums, however, the predominant vocabulary of images is the one provided by the older art of princes, but its meaning is no longer that of illustrating the actual life of princes but rather that of symbolizing a good and happy life. The motifs, therefore, do not have to be taken literally. Next to princely and narrative themes there are depictions of scenes of daily life, astronomical motifs, and a myriad of topics that can be described but not understood.

The main identifiable group of miniature painters is the so-called Baghdad school of the first half of the 13th century. The group should be called the Arab school because the subject matter and style employed could have been identified with any one of the major artistic centres of Egypt and the Fertile Crescent, and very little evidence currently exists to limit this school to one city. The miniatures painted by these artists are characterized by the colourful and often humorous way in which the urbanized Arab is depicted. The compositions, often lacking in any strong aesthetic intent, are documentary caricatures in which the artist has recorded the telling and recognizable gesture or a known and common setting or activity. In many images or compositional devices, one can recognize the impact of the richer Christian Mediterranean tradition of manuscript illumination. A greater attention to aesthetic considerations is apparent in the illustrated manuscript of the Persian epic *Varqeh o-Golshāh*, unique in the Seljuq period.

While it is possible within certain limits to generalize about the subject matter of Seljuq art, regional stylistic definitions tend to be more valid. Thus, the bronzes produced in northeastern Iran in the 12th century are characterized by simple decorative compositions rather than by the very elaborate ones created by the so-called school

This bowl from Kāshān, Iran, dates to the late 14th century. Kāshān ware drew on motifs in earlier textiles and is especially noted for the density and delicate execution of its decorative patterns.

of Mosul in Iraq during the 13th century. In general, the art of metalwork exhibits a consistently growing intricacy in composition and in details to the point that individual subjects are at times lost in overlapping planes of arabesques. Ceramic pieces of Iran have usually been classified according to a more or less fictitious provenance. Kāshān ware exhibits a perfection of line in the depiction of moon-faced personages with heavily patterned clothes, while Rayy ceramic work is less sophisticated in design and execution but more vividly coloured. Sāveh and Gurgān are still other Iranian varieties of pottery. With the exception of Kāshān ware, where dynasties of ceramicists are known, all these types of Iranian pottery were contemporary with each other. In Syria, Raqqah pottery imitated Iranian ceramic wares but with a far more limited vocabulary of designs.

Western Islamic Art: Moorish

The 11th to 13th centuries were not peaceful in the Maghrib. Amazigh (Berber) dynasties overthrew each other in Morocco and the Iberian Peninsula. The Christian Reconquista gradually diminished Muslim holdings in Spain and Portugal, and Tunisia was ruined during the Hilālī invasion when Bedouin tribes were sent by the Fāṭimids to prevent local independence.

Two types of structures characterize the Almoravid (1056–1147) and Almohad (1130–1269) periods in Morocco and Spain. One comprises the large, severely designed Moroccan mosques such as those of Tinmel, of Ḥasan in Rabat, or of the Kutubiyyah (Koutoubia) in Marrakech. They are all austere hypostyles with tall, massive, square minarets. The other distinctive type of architecture was that built for military purposes, including fortifications and, especially, massive city gates with low-slung horseshoe arches, such as the Oudaia Gate at Rabat (12th century) or the Rabat Gate at Marrakech (12th century). Palaces built in central Algeria by minor dynasties such as the Zīrids were more in the Fāṭimid tradition of Egypt than in the Almoravid and Almohad traditions of western Islam. Almost nothing is known or has been studied about North African arts other than architecture, because the puritanical world of the Berber dynasties did not foster the arts of luxury.

In North Africa the artistic milieu did not change much in the 14th and 15th centuries. Hypostyle mosques such as the Great Mosque of Algiers continued to be built. Madrasahs were constructed with more elaborate plans; the Bū ʿInānīyah madrasah at Fès is one of the few monumental buildings of the period. A few mausoleums were erected, such as the so-called Marīnid tombs near Fès (second half of the 14th century) or the complex of Chella at Rabat (mostly 14th century). Architectural decoration in stucco or sculpted stone was usually limited to elaborate geometric patterns, epigraphic themes, and a few vegetal motifs.

A stunning exception to the austerity of North African architecture exists in Spain in the Alhambra palace complex at Granada. The hill site of the Alhambra had been occupied by a citadel and possibly by a palace since the 11th century, but little of those earlier constructions has remained. In the 14th century two successive princes, Yūsuf I and Muḥammad V, transformed the hill into their official residence.

The Fuente de los Leones (Fountain of the Lions) stands at the centre of the Patio de los Leones (Court of the Lions), one of the principal courts at the Alhambra.

Outside of a number of gates built like triumphal arches and several ruined forecourts, only three parts of the palace remain intact. First there is the long Court of the Myrtles, leading to the huge Hall of the Ambassadors, located in one of the exterior towers. This was the part of the Alhambra built by Yūsuf I. Then there is the Court of the Lions, with its celebrated lion fountain in the centre. Numerous rooms open off this court, including the elaborately decorated Hall of the Two Sisters and the Hall of the Abencerrajes. The third part, slightly earlier than the first two, is the Generalife; it is a summer residence built higher up the hill and surrounded by gardens with fountains, pavilions, and portico walks.

The Alhambra is especially important because it is one of the few palaces to have survived from the medieval Islamic period. It illustrates superbly a number of architectural concerns occasionally documented in literary references: the contrast between an unassuming exterior and a richly decorated interior to achieve an effect of secluded or private brilliance; the constant presence of water, either as a single, static basin or as a dynamic fountain; the inclusion of oratories and baths; and the lack of an overall plan (the units are simply attached to each other).

The architectural decoration of the Alhambra was mostly of stucco. Some of it is flat, but the extraordinarily complex cupolas of muqarnas, as in the Hall of the Two Sisters, appear as huge multifaceted diadems. The decoration of the Alhambra becomes a sort of paradox as well as a tour de force. Weighty, elaborately decorated ceilings, for example, are supported by frail columns or by walls pierced with many windows (light permeates almost every part of the large, domed halls). Much of the design and decoration of the Alhambra is symbolically oriented. The poems that adorn the Alhambra as calligraphic ornamentation celebrate its cupolas as domes of heaven rotating around the prince sitting under them.

Islamic art as such ceased to be produced in Spain after 1492, when Granada, the last Moorish kingdom in Spain, fell to the Christians, but the Islamic tradition continued in North Africa, which remained Muslim. In Morocco the so-called Sharīfian dynasties from the 16th century onward ornamentally developed the artistic forms created in the 14th century.

Most of the best-known monuments of western Islamic art are buildings, although a very original calligraphy was developed. The other arts cannot be compared in wealth and importance either to what occurred elsewhere in Islam at the same time or to earlier objects created in Spain. There are some fine examples of metalwork, wood inlaid with ivory, and a lustre-glaze pottery known as Hispano-Moresque ware. The fact that the latter was made in Valencia or Málaga after the termination of Muslim rule demonstrates that Islamic traditions in the decorative arts continued to be adhered to, if only partially. The term Mudéjar, therefore, is used to refer to all the things made in a Muslim style but under Christian rule. Many examples of Mudéjar art exist in ceramics and textiles, as well as in architectural monuments such as the synagogues of Toledo and the Alcazba in Sevilla (Seville), where even the name of the ruling Christian prince, Don Pedro, was written in Arabic letters. The Mudéjar spirit, in fact, permeated most of Spanish architectural ornament and decorative arts for centuries, and its influence can even be found in Spanish America.

Mudéjar art must be carefully distinguished from Mozarabic art, the art of Christians under Muslim rule. Mozarabic art primarily flourished in Spain during the earlier periods of Muslim rule. Its major manifestations are architectural decorations, decorative objects, and illuminated manuscripts. Dating mostly from the 10th and 11th centuries, the celebrated illuminations for the commentary on the Revelation to John by an 8th-century Spanish abbot, Beatus of Liébana, are purely Christian subjects treated in styles possibly influenced by

Muslim miniature painting or book illustration. The most-celebrated example, known as the *Saint-Sever Apocalypse*, is in the collection of the Bibliothèque Nationale in Paris.

Mamlūk Art

The Mamlūks were originally slaves, chiefly Turks and Circassians from the Caucasus and Central Asia, who formed the mercenary army of the various feudal states of Syria and Egypt. During the 13th century the importance of this military caste grew as the older feudal order weakened and military commanders took over power, generally as nonhereditary sultans. They succeeded in arresting the Mongol onslaught in 1260 and, through a judicious but complicated system of alliance with the urban elite class, managed to maintain themselves in power in Egypt, Palestine, and Syria until 1517.

During the Mamlūk period Egypt and Syria were rich commercial emporiums. This wealth explains the quality and quantity of Mamlūk art. Most of the existing monuments in the old quarters of Cairo, Damascus, Tripoli, and Aleppo are Mamlūk; in Jerusalem almost everything visible on the Ḥaram al-Sharīf, with the exception of the Dome of the Rock, is Mamlūk. Museum collections of Islamic art generally abound with Mamlūk metalwork and glass. Some of the oldest remaining carpets are Mamlūk. This creativity required, of course, more than wealth. It also required a certain will to transform wealth into art. This will was in part the desire of parvenu rulers and their cohorts to be remembered. Furthermore, architectural patronage flourished because of the institutionalization of the *waqf*, an economic system in which investments made for holy purposes were inalienable. This law allowed the wealthy to avoid confiscation of their properties at the whim of the caliph by investing their funds in religious institutions.

In the Mamlūk period, therefore, there was a multiplication of madrasahs, khānqāhs, ribāṭs, and mosques, often with tombs of founders attached to them. The Mamlūk establishment also repaired and kept up all the institutions, religious or secular, that had been inherited by them, as can be demonstrated by the well-documented repairs carried on in Jerusalem and Damascus.

Architecture

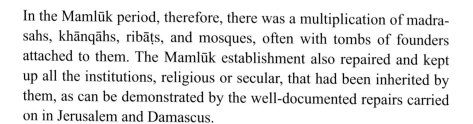

The Mamlūks created a monumental setting for Syria and Egypt that has lasted into the 21st century. It was at its most remarkable in architecture, and nearly 3,000 major monuments have been preserved or are known from texts in cities from the Euphrates to Cairo. No new architectural types came into being, although many more urban commercial buildings and private houses have been preserved than from previous centuries. The hypostyle form continued to be used for mosques and oratories, as in the Cairene mosques of Baybars I (1262–63), Nāṣir (1335), and Mu'ayyad Shaykh (1415–20). Madrasahs used eyvāns, and the justly celebrated madrasah of Sultan Ḥasan in Cairo (1356–62) is one of the few perfect four-eyvān madrasahs in the Islamic world. Mausoleums were squares or polygons covered with domes. In other words, there were only minor modifications in the typology of architecture, and even the 15th-century buildings with interiors totally covered with ornamentation have possible prototypes in the architecture of the Seljuqs. Yet there are formal and functional features that do distinguish Mamlūk buildings. One is the tendency to build structures of different functions in a complex or cluster. Thus, the Qalā'ūn mosque (1284–85) in Cairo has a mausoleum, a madrasah, and a hospital erected as one architectural unit. Another characteristic is the tendency of Mamlūk patrons to build their major monuments near each other. As a result, certain streets of Cairo, such as Bayn al-Qaṣrayn, became galleries of architectural masterpieces. The plans of those buildings may have had to be adapted to the exigencies of the city, but their spectacular facades and minarets competed with each other for effect. From the second half of the 14th century onward, building space for mausoleums began to be limited in Cairo, and a vast complex of commemorative monuments was created in the city's western cemetery. In Aleppo and Damascus similar phenomena can be observed.

Although Mamlūk architecture was essentially conservative in its development of building types, more originality is evident in the constructional systems used, although traditional structural features continued to be employed—e.g., cupolas raised on squinches, or more commonly, pendentives, barrel and groin vaults, and wooden ceilings covering large areas supported by columns and piers. The main

The Qalāʾūn complex was built in 1283–85 by the fifth Mamlūk sultan, Qalāʾūn. The hospital, now in ruins, was one of the most remarkable buildings of the Mamlūk era. The mausoleum and madrasah both open from a central corridor.

innovations are of three kinds. First, minarets became particularly elaborate and, toward the end of the period, almost absurd in their ornamentation. Facades were huge, with overwhelming portals 25 to 35 feet (7.5 to 10.5 metres) high.

A second characteristically Mamlūk feature was technical virtuosity in stone construction. At times this led to a superb purity of form, as in the Gate of the Cotton Merchants in Jerusalem or the complex of the Barqūq mosque in Cairo. At other times, as in the Mamlūk architecture of Baybars and Qāʾit Bāy, there was an almost wild playfulness with forms. Another aspect of Mamlūk masonry was the alternation of stones of different colours to provide variations on the surfaces of buildings.

The third element of change in Mamlūk art was perhaps the most important: almost all formal artistic achievements rapidly became part of the common vocabulary of the whole culture, thus ensuring high quality of construction and decorative technique throughout the period.

With the exception of portals and qiblah walls, architectural decoration was usually subordinated to the architectural elements of the design. Generally, the material of construction (usually stone) was carved with ornamental motifs. Stucco decoration was primarily used in early Mamlūk architecture, while coloured tile was a late decorative device that was rarely employed.

Other Arts

Like architecture, the other arts of the Mamlūk period achieved a high level of technical perfection without introducing major innovations. Mamlūk mosque lamps provide some of the finest examples of medieval glass. The wooden objects made by Mamlūk craftsmen

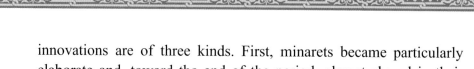

This lamp is from the Mosque-Madrasah of Sultan Ḥasan, in Cairo. The glassware of the Mamlūk era often featured enameled or gilded glass.

were widely celebrated for the quality of their painted, inlaid, or carved designs. And the bold inscriptions that decorate the hundreds of remaining bronzes testify to the Mamlūk mastery of calligraphy. The so-called *Baptistère de Saint Louis* (*c.* 1310) is the most impressive example of inlaid metalwork preserved from this period. Several Mamlūk illustrated manuscripts, such as the *Maqāmāt* (1334) in the National Library, Vienna, display an amazing ornamental sense in the use of colour on gold backgrounds.

Mongol Iran: Il-Khanid and Timurid Periods

Seen from the vantage point of contemporary or later chronicles, the 13th century in Iran was a period of destructive wars and invasions. Such cities as Balkh, Nīshāpūr, and Rayy, which had been centres of Islamic culture for nearly six centuries, were eradicated as the Mongol army swept through Iran. The turning point toward some sort of stability took place in 1295 with the accession of Maḥmūd Ghāzān to the Mongol throne. Under him and his successors (the Il-Khan dynasty), order was reestablished throughout Iran, and cities in northeastern Iran, especially Tabrīz and Solṭānīyeh, became the main creative centres of the new Mongol regime. At Tabrīz, for example, the Rashīdīyeh (a sort of academy of sciences and arts to which books, scholars, and ideas from all over the world were collected) was established in the early 14th century.

Under the Mongol rulers existed a number of secondary dynasties that flourished in various provinces of Iran: the Jalāyirid dynasty, centred in Baghdad, controlled most of western Iran; the Moẓaffarid dynasty of southwestern Iran contained the cities of Eṣfahān, Yazd, and Shīrāz; and the Karts reigned in Khorāsān. Until the last decade of the 14th century, however, all the major cultural centres were in western Iran. Under Timur (1336–1405) and his successors (the Timurid dynasty), however, northeastern Iran, especially the cities of Samarkand and Herāt, became focal points of artistic and intellectual activity. But Timurid culture affected the whole of Iran either directly or through minor local dynasties. Many Timurid monuments, therefore, are found in western or southern Iran.

ARCHITECTURE

Stylistically, Il-Khanid architecture is defined best by buildings such as the mosque of Varāmīn (1322–26) and the mausoleums at Sarakhs, Merv, Rād-Kān, and Marāgheh. In all those examples, the elements of architectural composition, decoration, and construction that had been developed earlier were refined by Il-Khanid architects. Eyvāns were shallower but better integrated with the courts, facades were more thoughtfully composed, the muqarnas became more linear and varied, and coloured tiles were used to enhance the building's character.

The architectural masterpiece of the Il-Khanid period is the mausoleum of Öljeitü at Solṭānīyeh. With its double system of galleries, eight minarets, large blue-tiled dome, and an interior measuring 80 feet (25 metres), it is clear that the building was intended to be imposing. Il-Khanid attention to impressiveness of scale also accounted for the ʿAlī Shāh mosque in Tabrīz, whose eyvān, measuring 150 by 80 by 100 feet (45 by 25 by 30 metres), was meant to be the largest ever built. The eyvān vault collapsed almost immediately after it had been constructed, but its walls, 35 feet (10 metres) thick, remain as a symbol of the grandiose taste of the Il-Khanids. In the regions of Eṣfahān and Yazd numerous smaller mosques (often with unusual plans) and less ostentatious mausoleums, as well as palaces with elaborate gardens, were built in the 14th century. Those buildings were constructed to

Completed in 1404, the Gūr-e Amīr was intended to be the tomb of Timur's grandson Muhammad Shah, but after Timur's death in 1405 he was interred there as well, along with other members of his family.

provide a monumental setting for the Islamic faith and to demonstrate the authority of the state.

The Timurid period began architecturally in 1390 with the sanctuary of Aḥmad Yasavī in Turkistan. Between 1390 and the last works of Sultan Ḥusayn Bāyqarā almost a century later, hundreds of buildings were constructed at Herāt, many of which have been preserved. The most spectacular examples of Timurid architecture are found in Samarkand, Herāt, Mashhad, Khargird, Tayābād, Baku, and Tabrīz, although important Timurid structures were also erected in southern Iran.

Architectural projects were well patronized by the Timurids as a means to commemorate their respective reigns. Every ruler or local governor constructed his own sanctuaries, mosques, and, especially, memorial buildings dedicated to holy men of the past. While the Shāh-e Zendah in Samarkand—a long street of mausoleums comparable to the Mamlūk cemetery of Cairo—is perhaps the most accessible of the sites of Timurid commemorative architecture, more spectacular ones are to be seen at Mashhad, Torbat-e Jām, and Mazār-e Sharīf. The Timurid princes also erected mausoleums for themselves, such as the Gūr-e Amīr and the ʿIshrat-Khāneh in Samarkand.

Major Timurid buildings—such as the mosque of Bībī Khānom and the Gūr-e Amīr mausoleum, both in Samarkand; the mosque of Gowhar Shād in Mashhad; or the madrasahs at Khargird and Herāt—are all characterized by strong axial symmetry. Often the facade on the inner court repeats the design of the outer facade, and minarets are used to frame the composition. Changes took place in the technique of dome construction. The muqarnas was not entirely abandoned but was often replaced by a geometrically rigorous net of intersecting arches that could be adapted to various shapes by modifying the width or span of the dome. The Khargird madrasah and the ʿIshrat-Khāneh mausoleum in Samarkand are particularly striking examples of this structural development. The Timurids also made use of double domes on high drums.

In the Timurid period the use of colour in architecture reached a high point. Every architectural unit was divided, on both the exterior and interior, into panels of brilliantly coloured tiles that sometimes were mixed with stucco or terra-cotta architectural decorations.

PAINTING

A new period of Persian painting began in the Mongol era; even though here and there one can recognize the impact of Seljuq painting, on the whole it is a limited one. Although the new style was primarily expressed in miniature painting, it is known from literary sources that mural painting flourished as well. Masterpieces of Persian literature were illustrated: first the *Shāh-nāmeh* ("Book of Kings") by the 11th-century poet Ferdowsī and then, from the second half of the 14th century, lyrical and mystical works, primarily those by the 12th-century poet Neẓāmī. Historical texts or chronicles such as Rashīd al-Dīn's *Jāmiʿ al-tawārīkh* ("The Collection of Chronicles") were also illustrated, especially in the early Mongol period.

The first major monument of Persian painting in the Mongol period is a group of manuscripts of the *Jāmiʿ al-tawārīkh*. The miniatures are historical narrative scenes. Stylistically, they are related to Chinese painting—an influence introduced by the Mongols during the Il-Khanid period.

Chinese influence can still be discovered in the masterpiece of 14th-century Persian painting, the so-called Demotte *Shāh-nāmeh* (named for the French dealer Georges Demotte who destroyed the binding in the early 20th century), also called the Great Mongol *Shāh-nāmeh*. Illustrated between 1320 and 1360, its 56 preserved miniatures have been dispersed all over the world. The compositional complexity of those paintings can be attributed to the fact that several painters probably were involved in the illustration of the manuscript and that the artists drew from a wide variety of different stylistic sources (e.g., Chinese, European, local Iranian traditions). Its main importance lies in the fact that it is the earliest known illustrative work that sought to depict in a strikingly dramatic fashion the meaning of the Iranian epic. Its battle scenes, its descriptions of fights with monsters, its enthronement scenes are all powerful representations of the colourful and often cruel legend of Iranian kingship. The artists also tried to express human powerlessness when confronted by fate in a series of mourning and death scenes.

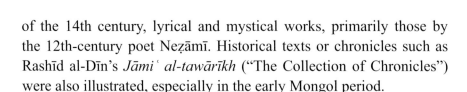

The Demotte *Shāh-nāmeh* is but the most remarkable of a whole series of 14th-century manuscripts, all of which suggest an art of painting in search of a coherent style. At the very end of the period, a manuscript such as that of the poems of Sultan Aḥmad still exhibits an effective variety of established themes, while some of the miniatures of the period illustrate the astounding variety of styles studied or copied by Persian masters.

A more organized and stylistically coherent period in Persian painting began about 1396 with the Khwāju Kermānī manuscript and culminated between 1420 and 1440 in the paintings produced by the Herāt school, an academy created by Timur's son Shāh Rokh and developed by Shāh Rokh's son Baysunqur Mīrzā to codify, copy, and illustrate classical Iranian literature. Although several *Shāh-nāmeh*s are known from this time, the mood of those manuscripts is no longer epic but lyrical. Puppetlike figures almost unemotionally engage in a variety of activities always set in an idealized garden or palace depicted against a rich gold background. It is a world of sensuous pleasure that also embodies the themes of a mystically interpreted lyrical poetry, for what is represented is not the real world but a divine paradise in the guise of a royal palace or garden. At its best, as in the illustrated manuscripts of Neẓāmī (Niẓāmī) held by New York City's Metropolitan Museum of Art, this style of Persian painting succeeds in defining something more than mere ornamental colourfulness. It expresses in its controlled lyricism a fascinating search for the divine, similar to the search of such epic characters as those presented in the works of Neẓāmī, Rūmī, or Ḥāfeẓ, at times earthly and vulgar, at other times quite ambiguous and hermetic, but often providing a language for the ways in which human beings can talk about God.

Another major change in Persian painting occurred during the second half of the 15th century at Herāt under Ḥusayn Bāyqarā. This change is associated with the first major painter of Islamic art, Behzād. Many problems of attribution are still posed about Behzād's art. In the examples that follow, works by his school, as well as images by the master's own hand, are included. In the Garrett *Ẓafar-nāmeh* (*c.* 1490, housed at Princeton University), the Egyptian Cairo National Library's *Būstān* (1488), or the British Museum's Neẓāmī

The Building of the Famous Castle of Khawarnaq is a miniature by Behzād. Dating from around 1494, it is an illustration for a collection of poems called the *Khamseh* of Neẓāmī. Today it is in the British Library, in London.

(1493–94), the stereotyped formulas of the earlier lyric style were endowed with new vitality. Behzād's interest in observing his environment resulted in the introduction of more realistic poses and the introduction of numerous details of daily life or genre elements. His works also reflect a concern for a psychological interpretation of the scenes and events depicted. It is thus not by chance that portraits have been attributed to Behzād.

Persian art of the Mongol period differs in a very important way from any of the other traditions of the middle period of Islamic art. Even though Iran, like all other areas at that time, was not ethnically homogeneous, its art tended to be uniquely "national." In architecture, nationalism was mostly a matter of function, for during this period the Shīʿites grew in importance, and new monumental settings were required for their holy places. Iranian individualism is especially apparent in painting, in which Chinese and other foreign styles were consistently adapted to express intensely Iranian subjects, thereby creating a uniquely Persian style.

CHAPTER 4

LATE PERIOD TO THE PRESENT DAY

The last period of an Islamic artistic expression created within a context of political and intellectual independence was centred in the Ottoman, Ṣafavid, and Mughal empires. Although culturally very different from each other, those three imperial states shared a common past and a common consciousness of the nature of their ancestry and of the artistic forms associated with it. Painters and architects moved from one empire to the other, especially from Iran to India; Ottoman princes wrote Persian poetry, and Ṣafavid rulers spoke Turkish. But most of all, they were aware of the fact that they were much closer to each other than to any non-Islamic cultural entity. However different their individual artistic forms may have been, they collected each other's works, exchanged gifts, and felt that they belonged to the same world.

OTTOMAN ART

The Ottomans were originally only one of the small Turkmen principalities (*beyliks*) that sprang up in Anatolia about 1300, after the collapse of Seljuq rule. In many ways, all the beyliks shared the same culture, but it was the extraordinary political and social attributes of the Ottomans that led them eventually to swallow up the other kingdoms, to conquer the Balkans, to take Constantinople (now Istanbul) in 1453, and to control almost the whole of the Arab world by 1520. Only in the 19th century did this complex empire begin to crumble. Thus, while Ottoman art, especially architecture, is best known through the monuments in Turkey, there is, in fact, evidence of Ottoman art extending from Algiers to Cairo in North Africa, to Damascus in the Levant, and in the Balkans from Sarajevo, Bosnia and Herzegovina to Sofia, Bulgaria.

ARCHITECTURE

The grand tradition of Ottoman architecture, established in the 16th century, was derived from two main sources. One was the rather complex development of new architectural forms that occurred all over Anatolia, especially at Manisa, İznik, Bursa, and Selçuk in the 14th and early 15th centuries. In addition to the usual mosques, mausoleums, and madrasahs, a number of buildings called *tekke*s (Arabic *zāwiyah*s, Persian khānqāhs) were constructed to house dervishes (members of mystical fraternities) and other holy men who lived communally. The *tekke* (or *zeviye*) was often joined to a mosque or mausoleum. The entire complex was then called a *külliye*. All those buildings continued to develop the domed, central-plan structure constructed by the Seljuqs in Anatolia.

The other source of Ottoman architecture is Christian art. The Byzantine tradition, especially as embodied in Hagia Sophia, became a major source of inspiration. Byzantine influence appears in such features as stone and brick used together or in the use of pendentive dome construction. Also artistically influential were the contacts that the early Ottomans had with Italy. Thus, in several mosques at Bursa, Turkey, there are stylistic parallels in the designs of the exterior facade and of windows, gates, and roofs to features found in

Italian architecture. A distinctive feature of Ottoman architecture is that it drew from both Islamic and European artistic traditions and was, therefore, a part of both.

The apogee of Ottoman architecture was achieved in the great series of külliyes and mosques that still dominate the Istanbul skyline: the Fatih külliye (1463–70), the Bayezid Mosque (after 1491), the Selim Mosque (1522), the Şehzade külliye (1548), and the Süleyman külliye (after 1550). The Şehzade and Süleyman külliyes were built by Sinan, the greatest Ottoman architect, whose masterpiece is the Selim Mosque at Edirne, Turkey (1569–75). All those buildings exhibit total clarity and logic in both plan and elevation; every part has been considered in relation to the whole, and each architectural element has acquired a hierarchic function in the total composition. Whatever is unnecessary has been eliminated. This simplicity of design in the late 15th and 16th centuries has often been attributed to the fact that Sinan and many other Ottoman architects were first trained as military engineers. Everything in those buildings was subordinated to an imposing central dome. A sort of cascade of descending half domes, vaults, and ascending buttresses leads the eye up and down the building's exterior. Minarets, slender and numerous, frame the exterior composition, while the open space of the surrounding courts prevents the building from being swallowed by the surrounding city. These masterpieces of Ottoman architecture seem to be the final perfection of two great traditions: a stylistic and aesthetic tradition that had been indigenous to Istanbul since the construction of the Byzantine church of Hagia Sophia in the 6th century and the other Islamic tradition of domical construction dating to the 10th century.

The tragedy of Ottoman architecture is that it never managed to renew its 16th-century brilliance. Later buildings, such as the impressive Sultan Ahmed mosque in Istanbul, were mostly variations on Sinan's architecture, and sometimes there were revivals of older building types, especially in the provinces. Occasionally, as in the early 18th-century Nûruosman mosque in Istanbul, interesting new variants appear illustrating the little-known Turkish Baroque style. The latter, however, is more visible in ornamental details or in smaller buildings, especially the numerous fountains built in Istanbul in the 18th century. The sources of the Turkish Baroque are probably to be sought in the Baroque architecture of Vienna and the bordering Austro-Hungarian states. Throughout the 18th and 19th centuries, a consistent Europeanization of a local tradition occurs in the Ottoman Empire.

While mosques and külliyes are the most characteristic monuments of Ottoman architecture, important secular buildings were also built: baths, caravansaries, and especially the huge palace complex

The Selim Mosque dominates the skyline of Edirne, Turkey. The mosque forms an architectural whole, with adjacent complementary buildings, including a school, library, and theological college.

of Topkapı Saray at Istanbul, in which 300 years of royal architecture are preserved in its elaborate pavilions, halls, and fountains.

Other Arts

Architectural decoration was generally subordinated to the structural forms or architectonic features of the building. A wide variety of themes and techniques originating from many different sources were used. One decorative device, the Ottoman version of colour tile decoration, deserves particular mention, for it succeeds in transforming smaller buildings such as the mosque of Rüstem Paşa in Istanbul into a visual spectacle of brilliant colours. The history and development of this type of ceramic decoration is intimately tied to the complex and much-controverted problem of the growth of several distinctive Ottoman schools of pottery: İznik, Rhodian, and Damascus ware. Both in technique and in design, Ottoman ceramics are the only major examples of pottery produced in the late Islamic period.

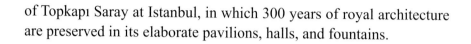

İznik ware was painted with stylized and symmetrical designs of flowers, leaves, and fruits, along with scenes with boats or animals and abstract linear motifs based on natural forms.

Ottoman miniature painting does not compare in quality to Persian painting, which originally influenced the Turkish school. Yet Ottoman miniatures do have a character of their own, either in the almost folk art effect of religious images or in the precise depictions of such daily events as military expeditions or great festivals. Among the finest examples of the latter is the manuscript *Surname-i Vehbi* painted by Abdülcelil Levnî in the early 18th century.

The production of metalwork, wood inlaid with ivory, Ushak carpets, and textiles flourished under the Ottomans, both in Istanbul workshops sponsored by the sultan and in numerous provincial centres. The influence of those ornamental objects on European decorative arts from the 16th through the 19th century was considerable.

ṢAFAVID ART

The Ṣafavid dynasty was founded by Ismāʿīl I (ruled 1501–24). The art of this dynasty was especially noteworthy during the reigns of Ṭahmāsp I (1524–76) and ʿAbbās I (1588–1629). This phase of the Ṣafavid period also marked the last significant development of Islamic art in Iran, for after the middle of the 17th century original creativity disappeared in all mediums. Rugs and objects in silver, gold, and enamel continued to be made and exhibited a considerable technical virtuosity, even when they were lacking in inventiveness.

The Ṣafavids abandoned Central Asia and northeastern Iran to a new Uzbek dynasty that maintained the Timurid style in many buildings (especially at Bukhara) and briefly sponsored a minor and derivative school of painting. Only the great sanctuary of Mashhad was being kept up and built up, but, like many of the other religious sanctuaries of the time—Qom, Al-Najaf, Karbalāʾ—it is still far too little known to lend itself to coherent analysis. This was the time when Shīʿism became a state religion, and for the first time in Islam there appeared an organized ecclesiastical system rather than the more or less loose spiritual and practical leadership of old. The main centres of the Ṣafavid empire were Tabrīz and Ardabīl in the northwest, with Kazvin in the central region and, especially, Eṣfahān in the west. The Ṣafavid period, like the

Ottoman era, was an imperial age, and therefore there is hardly a part of Iran where either Ṣafavid buildings or major Ṣafavid restorations cannot be found. The dynasty spent much money and effort on the building of bridges, roads, and caravansaries to encourage trade.

Architecture

The best-known Ṣafavid monuments are located at Eṣfahān, where ʿAbbās I built a whole new city. According to one description, it contained 162 mosques, 48 madrasahs, 1,802 commercial buildings, and 283 baths. Most of those buildings no longer survive, but the structures that remain constitute some of the finest monuments of Islamic architecture.

At the centre of Eṣfahān is the Maydān-e Shāh (now Maydān-e Emām), a large open space, about 1,670 by 520 feet (510 by 158 metres), originally surrounded by trees. Used for polo games and parades, it could be illuminated with 50,000 lamps. Each side of the *maydān* was provided with the monumental facade of a building. On one of the smaller sides was the entrance to a large mosque, the celebrated Masjed-e Shāh (now Masjed-e Emām). On the other side was the entrance into the bazaar or marketplace. On the longer sides were the small funerary mosque of Shaykh Luṭf Allāh and, facing it, the ʿAlī Qāpū, the "Lofty Gate," the first unit of a succession of palaces and gardens that extended beyond the maydān, most of which have now disappeared except for the Chehel Sotūn ("Forty Columns"), a palace built as an audience hall. The ʿAlī Qāpū was, in its lower floors, a semipublic place to which petitions could be brought, while its upper floors were a world of pure fantasy—a succession of rooms, halls, and balconies overlooking the city, which were purely for the prince's pleasure.

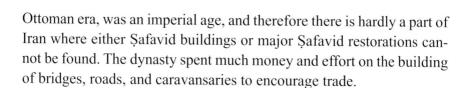

Along with the three neighbouring structures of the period, the Masjed-e Emām is notable for its logically precise vaulting and inventive use of coloured tiles.

The Maydān-e Emām unites in a single composition all the concerns of medieval Islamic architecture: prayer, commemoration, princely pleasure, trade, and spatial effect. None of the hundreds of other remaining Ṣafavid monuments can match its historical importance, and in it also are found the major traits of Ṣafavid construction and decoration. The forms are traditional, for the most part, and, even in vaulting techniques and the use of coloured tiles, it is to Timurid art that the Ṣafavids looked for their models. The Persian architects of the early 17th century sought to achieve a monumentality in exterior spatial composition (an interesting parallel to the interior spaciousness created at the same time by the Ottomans); a logical precision in vaulting, which was successful in the Masjed-e Emām but rapidly led to cheap effects or to stucco imitations; and a coloristic brilliance that has made the domes and portals of Eṣfahān justly famous.

Painting

In the 16th and 17th centuries, possibly for the first time in Islamic art, painters were conscious of historical styles—even self-conscious. Miniatures from the past were collected, copied, and imitated. Patronage, however, was fickle. A royal whim would gather painters together or exile them. Many names of painters have been preserved, and there is little doubt that the whim of patrons was being countered by the artists' will to be socially and economically independent as well as individually recognized for their artistic talents. Too many different impulses, therefore, existed in Ṣafavid Iran for painting to follow any clear line of development.

Three major painting styles, or schools (excluding a number of interesting provincial schools), existed in the Ṣafavid period. One school of miniature painting is exemplified by such masterpieces as the Houghton *Shāh-nāmeh* (completed in 1537), the Jāmī *Haft owrang* (1556–1665), and the illustrations to stories from Ḥāfeẓ. However different they are from each other, those large, colourful miniatures all were executed in a grand manner. Their compositions are complex, individual faces appear in crowded masses, there is much diversification in landscape, and, despite a few ferocious details of monsters or of strongly caricaturized poses and expressions, these book illustrations are concerned with an idealized vision of life. The sources of this school lie with the Timurid academy. Behzād, Sulṭān Muḥammad, Sheykhzādeh, Mīr Sayyid ʿAlī, Āqā Mīrak, and Maḥmūd Muṣavvīr continued and modified, each in his own way, the ideal of a balance between an overall composition and precise rendering of details.

Reẕā ʿAbbāsī's miniature *Khosrow Makes His Elephant Trample the Enemy* was an illustration for a 17th-century copy of the poet Neẓāmī's epic romance *Khosrow o-Shīrīn.*

The miniatures of the second tradition of Ṣafavid painting seem at first to be like a detail out of the work of the previously discussed school. The same purity of colour, elegance of poses, interest in details, and assertion of the individual figure is found. Āqā Reẕā and Reẕā ʿAbbāsī (both active in the late 16th and early 17th century) excelled in these extraordinary portrayals of poets, musicians, courtiers, and aristocratic life in general.

In both traditions of painting, the beautiful personages depicted frequently are satirized; this note of satirical criticism is even more pronounced in portraiture of the time. But it is in pen or brush drawings, mostly dating from the 17th century, that the third aspect of Ṣafavid painting appeared: an interest in genre, or the depiction of minor events of daily life (e.g., a washerwoman at work, a tailor sewing, an animal). With stunning precision, Ṣafavid artists showed a whole society falling apart with a cruel sympathy totally absent from the literary documents of the time.

While architecture and painting were the main artistic vehicles of the Ṣafavids, the making of textiles and carpets was also of great importance. It is in the 16th century that a hitherto primarily nomadic and folk medium of the decorative arts was transformed into an expression of royal and urban tasks by the creation of court workshops. The predominantly geometric themes of earlier Iranian carpets were not abandoned entirely but tended to be replaced by vegetal, animal, and even occasional human motifs. Great schools of carpet making developed particularly at Tabrīz, Kāshañ, and Kermān.

Mughal Art

The art of the Mughals was intimately connected with the indigenous Hindu traditions of the Indian subcontinent. However, it also has connections to Islamic art of the same period. It was similar to that of the Ottomans in that it was a late imperial art of Muslim princes. Both styles were rooted in several centuries (at least from the 13th century onward) of adaptation of Islamic functions to indigenous forms. It was in the 14th-century architecture of South Asian sites such as Tughluqabad, Gaur, and Ahmadabad that a uniquely Indian type of Islamic hypostyle mosque was created, with a triple axial nave, corner towers, axial minarets, and cupolas. It was also during those centuries that the first mausoleums set in scenically spectacular locations were built. By then the conquering Muslims had fully learned how to utilize local methods of construction, and they adapted South Asian decorative techniques and motifs.

Mughal art was in continuous contact with Iran or, rather, with the Timurid world of the second half of the 15th century. The models and the memories were in Herāt or Samarkand, but the artists were raided from Ṣafavid Iran, and the continuous flow of painters from Iran to the Mughal Empire is a key factor in understanding Mughal painting.

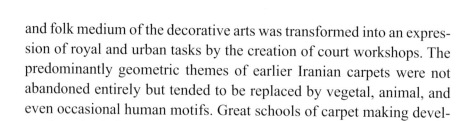

ARCHITECTURE

The advent of the Mughal dynasty marks a striking revival of Islamic architecture in northern India. Persian, Indian, and the various provincial styles were successfully fused to produce works of unusual refinement and quality. The tomb of Humāyūn, begun in 1564, inaugurates the new style. Built entirely of red sandstone and marble, it shows considerable Persian influence. The great fort at Āgra (1565–74) and the city of Fatehpur Sīkri (1569–74) represent the building activities of the emperor Akbar. The former has the massive so-called Delhi gate (1566) and lengthy and immense walls carefully designed and faced with dressed stone throughout. The most important achievements, however, are to be found at Fatehpur Sīkri; the Jāmiʿ Masjid (1571), with the colossal gateway known as the Buland Darwāza, for example, is one of the finest mosques of the Mughal period. Other notable buildings include the palace of Jodhā Bāl, which has a strongly indigenous aspect; the exquisitely carved Turkish Sultānā's house; the Pānch-Maḥal; the Dīvān-e ʿĀmm; and the so-called hall of private audience. Most of the buildings are of post and lintel construction, arches being used very sparingly. The tomb of the emperor, at Sikandarā, near Āgra, is of unique design, in the shape of a truncated square pyramid 340 feet (103 metres) on each side. It consists of five terraces, four of red sandstone and the uppermost of white marble. Begun about 1602, it was completed in 1613, during the reign of Akbar's son Jahāngīr. Architectural undertakings in this emperor's reign were not very ambitious, but there are fine buildings, chiefly at Lahore. The tomb of his father-in-law Iʿtimāẖ-ud-Dawla, at Āgra, is small but of exquisite workmanship, built entirely of delicately inlaid marble.

The reign of Shāh Jahān (1628–58) is as remarkable for its architectural achievements as was that of Akbar. He built the great Red Fort at Delhi (1639–48), with its dazzling hall of public audience, the flat roof of which rests on rows of columns and pointed, or cusped, arches, and the Jāmiʿ Masjid (1650–56), which is among the finest mosques in India. But it is the Tāj Mahal (*c.*1632–*c.* 1649), built as a tomb for Queen Mumtāz Maḥal, that is the greatest masterpiece of his reign. All the resources of the empire were put into its construction. In addition to the mausoleum proper, the complex included a wide variety of accessory buildings of great beauty. The marble mausoleum rises up from a tall terrace (at the four corners of which are elegant towers, or minārs) and is crowned by a graceful dome. Other notable buildings of

In its harmonious proportions and its fluid incorporation of decorative elements, the Taj Mahal is distinguished as the finest example of Mughal architecture, blending Indian, Persian, and Islamic styles.

the reign of Shāh Jahān include the Motī Masjid (*c.* 1648–55) and the Jāmiʿ Masjid at Āgra (1548–55).

Architectural monuments of the reign of Aurangzeb represent a distinct decline; the tomb of Rābīʿah Begam at Aurangābād, for example (1679), is a poor copy of the Tāj Mahal. The royal mosque at Lahore (1673–74) is of much better quality, retaining the grandeur and dignity of earlier work; and the Motī Masjid at Delhi (1659–60) possesses much of the early refinement and delicacy. The tomb of Ṣafdar Jang at Delhi (*c.* 1754) was among the last important works to be produced under the Mughal dynasty and had already lost the coherence and balance characteristic of mature Mughal architecture.

Painting

Although the Mughal dynasty came to power in India with the great victory won by Bābar at the Battle of Pānīpat in 1526, the Mughal style was almost exclusively the creation of Akbar. Trained in painting at an early age by a Persian master, Khwāja ʿAbd-uṣ-Ṣamad, who was employed by his father, Humāyūn, Akbar created a large atelier, which he staffed with artists recruited from all parts of India. The atelier, at least in the initial stages, was under the superintendence of Akbar's teacher and another great Persian master, Mīr Sayyid ʿAlī; but the distinctive style that evolved here owed not a little to the highly individual tastes of Akbar himself, who took an interest in the work, inspecting the atelier frequently and rewarding painters whose work was pleasing.

The earliest paintings (*c.* 1560–70) of the school of Akbar are illustrations of *Ṭūṭī-nāmeh* ("Parrot Book;" Cleveland Museum of Art) and the stupendous illustrations of the *Dāstān-e Amīr Ḥamzeh* ("Stories of Amīr Ḥamzeh;" Österreichisches Museum für Angewandte Kunst, Vienna), which originally consisted of 1,400 paintings of an unusually large size (approximately 25 inches by 16 inches [65 by 40 centimetres]), of which only about 200 have survived. The *Ṭūṭī-nāmeh* shows the Mughal style in the process of formation: the hand of artists belonging to the various non-Mughal traditions is clearly recognizable, but the style also reveals an intense effort to cope with the demands of a new patron. The transition is achieved in the *Dāstān-e Amīr Ḥamzeh*, in which the uncertainties are overcome in a homogeneous style, quite unlike Persian work in its leaning toward naturalism and filled with swift, vigorous movement and bold colour. The forms are individually modelled, except for the geometrical ornament used as architectural decor; the figures are superbly interrelated in closely unified compositions, in which depth is indicated by a preference for diagonals; and much attention is paid to the expression of emotion. One of the last manifestations of this bold and vigorous early manner is the *Dārāb-nameh (c.* 1580) in the British Museum.

Immediately following were some very important historical manuscripts, including the *Tārīkh-e Khāndān-e Tīmūrīyeh* ("History of the House of Timūr," *c.* 1580–85; Khuda Baksh Library, Patna) and other works concerned with the affairs of the Tīmūrid dynasty, to which the Mughals belonged. Each of these manuscripts contains several hundred illustrations, the prolific output of the atelier made possible by the division of labour that was in effect. Historical events are recreated with remarkable inventiveness, though the explosive and almost frantic energy of the *Dāstān-e Amīr-Ḥamzeh* has begun to subside. The scale was smaller and the work began to acquire a studied richness. The narrative method employed by these Mughal paintings, like that of traditional literature, is infinitely discursive; and the painter did not hesitate to provide a fairly detailed picture of contemporary life—both of the people and of the court—and of the rich fauna and

THE MUGHAL ATELIER

The work of the Mughal atelier in this early formative stage was largely confined to the illustration of books on a wide variety of subjects: histories, romances, poetic works, myths, legends, and fables, of both Indian and Persian origin. The manuscripts were first written by calligraphers, with blank spaces left for the illustrations. These were executed largely by groups of painters, including a colourist, who did most of the actual painting, and specialists in portraiture and in the mixing of colours. Chief of the group was the designer, generally an artist of top quality, who formulated the composition and sketched in the rough outline. A thin wash of white, through which the initial drawing was visible, was then applied and the colours filled in. The colourist's work proceeded slowly, the colour being applied in several thin layers and frequently rubbed down with an agate burnisher, a process that resulted in the glowing, enamel-like finish. The colours used were mostly mineral but sometimes consisted of vegetable dyes; and the brushes, many of them exceedingly fine, were made from squirrel's tail or camel hair.

flora of India. Like Indian artists of all periods, the Mughal painter showed a remarkable empathy for animals, for through them flows the same life that flows through human beings. This sense of kinship allowed him to achieve unqualified success in the illustration of animal fables such as the *Anwār-e Suhaylī* ("Lights of Caropus"), of which several copies were painted, the earliest dated 1570 (School of Oriental and African Studies, London). It was in the illustrations to Persian translations of the Hindu epics, the *Mahābhārata* and the *Rāmāyaṇa*, that the Mughal painter revealed to the full the richness of his imagination and his unending resourcefulness. With little precedent to rely on, he was nevertheless seldom dismayed by the subject and created a whole series of convincing compositions. Because most of the painters of the atelier were Hindus, the subjects must have been close to their hearts; and, given the opportunity by a tolerant and sympathetic patron, they rose to great heights. It is no wonder, therefore, that the *Razm-nāmeh* (City Palace Museum, Jaipur), as the *Mahābhārata* is known in Persian, is one of the outstanding masterpieces of the age.

In addition to large books containing numerous illustrations, which were the products of the combined efforts of many artists, the imperial atelier also cultivated a more intimate manner that specialized in the illustration of books, generally poetic works, with a smaller number of illustrations. The paintings were done by a single master artist who, working alone, had ample scope to display his virtuosity. In style the works tend to be finely detailed and exquisitely coloured. A *Dīvān* ("Anthology") of Anwarī (Fogg Art Museum, Cambridge, Massachusetts), dated 1589, is a relatively early example of this manner. The paintings are very small, none larger than five inches by $2^1/_2$ inches (12 by 6 centimetres) and most delicately executed. Very similar in size and quality are the miniatures illustrating the *Dīvān* of Ḥāfeẓ (Reza Library, Rāmpur). On a larger scale but in the same mood are the manuscripts that represent the most delicate and refined works of the reign of Akbar: the *Bahāristān* of Jāmī (1595; Bodleian Library, Oxford), a *Khamseh* of Neẓāmī (1593; British Museum, London), a *Khamseh* of Amīr Khosrow (1598; Walters Art Gallery, Baltimore and Metropolitan Museum of Art, New York), and an *Anwār-e Suhaylī* (1595–96; Bharat Kala Bhavan, Vārānasī).

Of the large number of painters who worked in the imperial atelier, the most outstanding were Dasvant and Basāvan. The former played the leading part in the illustration of the *Razm-nāmeh*. Basāvan, who is preferred by some to Dasvant, painted in a very distinctive style, which delighted in the tactile and the plastic, and

This painting of a bird perched on rocks dates from around 1610, during the reign of Jahāngīr. Today the painting is in the State Museum, in Hyderabad, India.

with an unerring grasp of psychological relationships.

The emperor Jahāngīr, even as a prince, showed a keen interest in painting and maintained an atelier of his own. His tastes, however, were not the same as those of his father, and this is reflected in the painting, which underwent a significant change. The tradition of illustrating books began to die out, though a few manuscripts, in continuation of the old style, were produced. For Jahāngīr much preferred portraiture; and this tradition, also initiated in the reign of his father, was greatly developed. Among the most elaborate works of his reign are the great court scenes, several of which have survived, showing Jahāngīr surrounded by his numerous courtiers. These are essentially large-scale exercises in portraiture, the artist taking great pains to reproduce the likeness of every figure.

The compositions of these paintings have lost entirely the bustle and movement so evident in the works of Akbar's reign. The figures are more formally ordered, their comportment in keeping with the strict rules of etiquette enforced in the Mughal court. The colours are subdued and harmonious, the bright glowing palette of the Akbarī artist having been quickly abandoned. The brushwork is exceedingly fine. Technical virtuosity, however, is not all that was attained, for beneath the surface of the great portraits of the reign there is a deep and often spiritual understanding of the character of the person and the drama of human life.

Many of the paintings produced at the imperial atelier are preserved in the albums assembled for Jahāngīr and his son Shāh Jahān. The *Muraqqah-e Gulshan* is the most spectacular. There are assembled masterpieces from Iran, curiosities from Europe, works produced in the reign of Akbar, and many of the finest paintings of Jahāngīr's master painters, all surrounded by the most magnificent borders decorated with a wide variety of floral and geometrical designs. The album gives a fairly complete idea of Jahāngīr as a patron, collector, and connoisseur of the arts, revealing a person with a wide range of taste and a curious, enquiring mind.

Jahāngīr esteemed the art of painting and honoured his painters. His favourite was Abū al-Hasan, who was designated Nādir-uz-Zamān ("Wonder of the Age"). Several pictures by the master are known, among them a perceptive study of Jahāngīr looking at a portrait of his father. Also much admired was Ustād Manṣūr, designated Nādir-ul-ʿAṣr ("Wonder of the Time"), whose studies of birds and animals are unparalleled. Bishandās was singled out by the emperor as unique in the art of portraiture. Manohar, the son of Basāvan, Govardhan, and Daulat are other important painters of this reign.

Under Shāh Jahān, attention seems to have shifted to architecture, but painting in the tradition of Jahāngīr continued. The style, however, becomes noticeably rigid. The portraits are lacking the breath of life so evident in the work of Jahāngīr's time. The colouring is jewel-like in its brilliance, and the outward splendour quite dazzling. The best work is found in the *Shāhjahānnāmeh* ("History of Shāh Jahān") of the Windsor Castle Library and in several albums assembled for the emperor. Govardhan and Bichitra, who had begun their careers in the reign of Jahāngīr, were among the outstanding painters; several works by them are quite above the general level produced in this reign.

From the reign of Aurangzeb (1659–1707), a few pictures have survived that essentially continue the cold style of Shāh Jahān;

but the rest of the work is nondescript, consisting chiefly of an array of lifeless portraits, most of them the output of workshops other than the imperial atelier. Genre scenes, showing gatherings of ascetics and holy men, lovers in a garden or on a terrace, musical parties, carousals, and the like, which had grown in number from the reign of Shāh Jahān, became quite abundant. They sometimes show touches of genuine quality, particularly in the reign of Muḥammad Shāh (1719–48), who was passionately devoted to the arts. This revival, however, was momentary, and Mughal painting essentially came to an end during the reign of Shāh ʿĀlam II (1759–1806). The artists of this disintegrated court were chiefly occupied in reveries of the past, the best work, for whatever it is worth, being confined to copies of old masterpieces still in the imperial library. This great library was dispersed and destroyed during the uprising of 1857 against the British.

Islamic Art Under European Influence and Contemporary Trends

It is difficult to decide when, how, and to what extent European art began to affect the art of the traditional Muslim world. Ottoman architecture was from the beginning affected by Western influences. In Mughal India, European landscapes and Western spatial concerns influenced painting in the 18th century. Persian painting has exhibited constant Western influence since the 17th century. Thus, Islamic art began to be affected by European traditions before Europe began (in the 18th and 19th centuries) its conquests of most of the Muslim world. Because the Ottomans ruled North Africa (except Morocco), Egypt, Syria, and Palestine, as well as the Balkans, much of the Muslim world was introduced to "modern" European art through its adaptation in Istanbul or in other major Ottoman cities such as Smyrna (now İzmir) or Alexandria.

European influence tended to have been mostly limited to architecture. Nineteenth-century European engineers and architects, for example, adapted modern structural technology and decorative styles to local Islamic needs or idioms: the Sūq al-Ḥamīdīyah bazaar in Damascus was built with steel roofing; the Hejaz railway station at Damascus was decorated in a sort of Eastern Art Nouveau style.

During actual European occupation of Muslim territory, there was a conscious revival of traditional decorative arts, but new techniques were often employed. This especially occurred in India and Morocco, where the retail success of an art object depended less on the local tradition than on the taste of the Europeans. What was romantic to a European, therefore, was no longer part of the world of the newly enriched and Europeanized Muslim. Much of the Europeanized architecture was drab and pretentious. The greatest artistic accomplishment of this period was in the preservation and encouragement of the traditional techniques and designs of the decorative arts, which often had to be maintained artificially through government subsidies.

During the period of occupation it was questioned whether alien techniques necessarily brought with them new forms. This mood was clearly expressed in literature but less so in the visual arts, because the quality of Muslim art had deteriorated so much in the decades preceding European arrival that there was no longer a lively creative force to maintain. As various schools based on the École des Beaux-Arts in Paris were formed, however, the faculties and the students suffered from constant uncertainty as to whether they should preserve an art that was mostly artisanal or revolutionize it altogether.

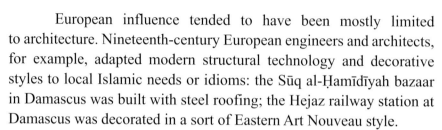

It is much more difficult to define in broad terms the characteristics of art in Muslim countries after the formation of independent countries in the 1940s and '50s. Extensive planning programs and building projects were undertaken in even the poorest countries, and the wealthy Arab states as well as prerevolutionary Iran transformed their traditional cities and countryside with spectacular modern complexes ranging from housing projects to universities. Many of those buildings were planned and constructed by Western firms and architects, and some are mere copies of European and American models, not necessarily adapted to the physical conditions and visual traditions of the Muslim world. Others are interesting and even sensitive projects: spectacular and technically innovative, such as the InterContinental Hotel in Mecca (designed by German architects Rolf Gutbrod and Frei Otto) and the Hajj Terminal at the King Abdulaziz International Airport at Jiddah, Saudi Arabia (designed by the US firm Skidmore, Owings & Merrill); or intelligent and imaginative, such as the government buildings of Dhaka, Bangladesh (designed by American architect Louis I. Kahn), or the numerous buildings designed by Frenchman André Ravereau in Mali and Algeria. Furthermore, within the Muslim world emerged several schools of architects that adopted modes of an international language to suit local conditions. The oldest of those schools are in Turkey.

Major Muslim contributors to a contemporary Islamic architecture include the Iranians Nader Ardalan and Kamran Diba, the Iraqis Rifat Chaderji and Mohamed Makiya, the Jordanian Rasem Badran, and the Bangladeshi Mazharul Islam. A unique message was transmitted by the visionary Egyptian architect Hassan Fathy, who, in eloquent and prophetic terms, urged that the traditional forms and techniques of vernacular architecture be studied and adapted to contemporary needs. Directly or indirectly, his work inspired many young architects in the Muslim world and led to a host of fascinating private houses, mosques, and educational facilities. The Aga Khan Award for Architecture was instituted to encourage genuine and contemporary architectural innovation in Muslim lands.

CONCLUSION

The 21st century has produced innovative art and architecture from the Islamic world, but has also been a period in which historically and artistically significant works, buildings, and monuments have been threatened and even destroyed. Some of the destruction was the unfortunate result of warfare in Iraq and Syria, though certain sites were targeted systematically. After the Islamic State in Iraq and the Levant (ISIL) took control of territory in Iraq and Syria in 2013 and 2014, it engaged in a campaign of cultural cleansing, destroying many ancient pre-Islamic artifacts and sites, as well as Shīʿite places of worship and Sunni shrines that it deemed idolatrous, such as the Mosque of the Prophet Jonah in Mosul.

Other parts of the Islamic world have seen positive developments for the arts. A new Museum of Islamic Art, located on the southern end of Doha Bay, in Qatar, opened in 2008. Designed by the Pritzker Prize-winning Chinese American architect I.M. Pei, the museum is noted for its vast collection of Islamic art spanning 1,300 years. In 2010 the redesigned Museum of Islamic Art in Cairo opened to visitors (the collection had swelled to more than 100,000 objects by 2003, making the exhibitions cramped and difficult for visitors to navigate).

There is also a diverse body of artists around the world creating new works to the field of Islamic art, drawing to various degrees on the traditions of Islamic art and global trends in contemporary art. Examples include the Iranian-born multimedia artist Shirin Neshat, whose work deals with Islam and gender relations; the Moroccan-born photographer Lalla Essaydi, known for her photographs of women overlaid with henna calligraphy; and the Egyptian-born Fathi Hassan, whose paintings and drawings often incorporate Arabic script. Art is and will doubtless continue to be an outlet for exploring the lives of the millions of people who live in or have roots in the Islamic world.

GLOSSARY

ARABESQUE A style of decoration characterized by intertwining plants and abstract curvilinear motifs. As adapted by Muslim artisans about 1000 CE, it became highly formalized.

ATELIER A workshop in which several people are employed at artists' or artisans' tasks.

ATAVISTIC Displaying a character typical of a more primitive ancestral form.

CUPOLA A small dome, often resembling an overturned cup, placed on a circular, polygonal, or square base or on small pillars or a glassed-in lantern. It is used to crown a turret, roof, or larger dome. The inner vault of a dome is also a cupola.

EPIGRAPHIC Relating to, consisting of, or bearing inscriptions.

HAGIOGRAPHY Idealizing or idolizing biography.

HETERODOX Differing from or contrary to an acknowledged standard, a traditional form, or an established religion. The opposite of orthodox.

HYPOSTYLE Having the roof resting on rows of columns.

ICONOCLASM Destroying religious images or being opposed to their veneration.

ICONOGRAPHY The imagery selected to convey the meaning of a work of art or the identity of its figures and setting and comprising figures or objects or features often fixed by convention; a set of symbolic forms.

MIHRAB The prayer niche in the *qiblah* wall (that facing Mecca) of a mosque.

MINARET In Islamic religious architecture, the tower from which the faithful are called to prayer five times each day by a muezzin, or crier.

MORPHOLOGICAL Of, relating to, or concerned with form or structure.

ORATORY A small, private place for prayer.

ORTHODOX Holding established beliefs, especially in religion. The opposite of heterodox.

PAPYRI Texts written on scrolls made of the pith of the papyrus plant.

PENDENTIVE A triangular segment of a spherical surface, filling in the upper corners of a room, in order to form, at the top, a circular support for a dome.

PORTICO A colonnaded porch or entrance to a structure, or a covered walkway supported by regularly spaced columns.

QIBLAH The direction of the sacred shrine of the Kaʿbah in Mecca, Saudi Arabia, toward which Muslims turn five times each day when performing the *salat* (daily ritual prayer).

SGRAFFITO A technique used in painting, pottery, and glass, which consists of putting down a preliminary surface, covering it with another, and then scratching the superficial layer in such a way that the pattern or shape that emerges is of the lower colour.

SLIP A layer of semiliquid clay, used in the production of pottery.

SPANDREL The roughly triangular area above and on either side of an arch, bounded by a line running horizontally through the apex of the arch, a line rising vertically from the springing of the arch, and the curved extrados, or top of the arch.

SQUINCH Any of several devices by which a square or polygonal room has its upper corners filled in to form a support for a dome.

STUCCO A plaster (as of portland cement, sand, and lime) used to cover exterior walls or ornament interior walls.

VEGETAL Having to do with plants or plant growth.

ZOOMORPHIC Having the form of often stylized animals.

BIBLIOGRAPHY

Theoretical discussions of Islamic art and architecture include Oleg Grabar, *The Formation of Islamic Art,* rev. and enlarged ed. (1987), and *The Mediation of Ornament: The A.W. Mellon Lectures in the Fine Arts* (1992); Nasser D. Khalili, *Visions of Splendour in Islamic Art and Culture* (2008; originally published as *The Timeline History of Islamic Art and Architecture*, 2005), and *Islamic Art and Culture: A Visual History* (2006); and Attilio Petruccioli and Khalil K. Pirani (eds.), *Understanding Islamic Architecture* (2002).

Among the excellent surveys of Islamic arts are Richard Ettinghausen, Oleg Grabar, and Marilyn Jenkins-Madina, *The Art and Architecture of Islam 650–1250*, 2nd ed. (2001); Sheila S. Blair and Jonathan M. Bloom, *The Art and Architecture of Islam 1250–1800* (1994); and Doris Behrens-Abouseif and Stephen Vernoit (eds.), *Islamic Art in the 19th Century: Tradition, Innovation, and Eclecticism* (2006). A four-volume survey that summarizes the author's work over many years is Oleg Grabar, *Early Islamic Art, 650–1100* (2005), *Islamic Visual Culture, 1100–1800* (2006), *Islamic Art and Beyond* (2006), and *Jerusalem* (2005). Other works include Titus Burckhardt, *Art of Islam: Language and Meaning* (1976; reissued in a commemorative edition, 2009) and Alexandre Papadopoulo, *Islam and Muslim Art* (1979, originally published in French, 1976). Leo A. Mayer, *Islamic Metalworkers and Their Works* (1959), *Islamic Architects and Their Works* (1956), and other similar titles, collect lists of artists.

A number of volumes treat many genres together. These include Barbara Brend, *Islamic Art* (1991); Ernest J. Grube et al., *Cobalt and Lustre: The First Centuries of Islamic Pottery* (1994); Nicola Barber, *Islamic Art & Culture* (2005); Nasser D. Khalili, *The Timeline History of Islamic Art and Architecture* (2005); Sheila R. Canby, *Islamic Art in Detail* (2005); Nasser D. Khalili, *Islamic Art and Culture: A Visual History* (2005); Jonathan Bloom, *Arts of the City Victorious: Islamic Art and Architecture in Fatimid North Africa and Egypt* (2007); and Jonathan Bloom (ed.), *Early Islamic Art and Architecture* (2000, reissued 2002).

Architecture

The built environment is discussed in John D. Hoag, *Islamic Architecture* (1976); George Michell (ed.), *Architecture of the Islamic World: Its History and Social Meaning* (1978); Nader Ardalan and Laleh Bakhtiar, *The Sense of Unity: The Sufi Tradition in Persian Architecture* (1973, reprinted 1979); and Sonia P. and Hans Christoph Seherr-Thoss, *Design and Color in Islamic Architecture: Afghanistan, Iran, Turkey* (1968).

Painting

Richard Ettinghausen, *Arab Painting* (1962); Basil Gray, *Persian Painting from Miniatures of the XIII–XVI Centuries* (1947); and Douglas E. Barrett and Basil Gray, *Painting of India* (1963, reissued 1978 as Indian Painting), discuss the role of painting. Also helpful are Oleg Grabar, *The Illustrations of the Maqamat* (1984); and J.M. Rogers, *Mughal Miniatures*, 2nd ed. (2006).

Metalwork

Good sources include R.M. Ward, *Islamic Metalwork* (1993); Eva Baer, *Metalwork in Medieval Islamic Art* (1983); Assadullah Souren Melikian-Chirvani, *Islamic Metalwork from the Iranian World, 8–18th Centuries* (1982); and James W. Allan, *Metalwork Treasures from the Islamic Courts* (2002), an exhibition catalogue.

Ceramics

For many years the key studies were Arthur Lane, *Early Islamic Pottery* (1947, reprinted 1965), and *Later Islamic Pottery,* 2nd ed.

(1971). Among the many later additions to scholarship on the subject are James W. Allan, *Islamic Ceramics* (1991); John Hedgecoe and Salma Samar Damluji (eds.), *Zillij: The Art of Moroccan Ceramics* (1992); John Carswell, *Iznik Pottery* (1998; reprinted 2007); Oliver Watson, *Ceramics from Islamic Lands* (2004); Walter B. Denny, *Iznik: The Artistry of Ottoman Ceramics* (2004); and Giovanni Curatola (ed.), *Persian Ceramics: From the 9th to the 14th Century* (2006).

CARPETS

Early scholarly studies on carpets are those of Kurt Erdmann, especially *Oriental Carpets* (1960, reissued 1976; originally published in German, 2nd ed., 1960), and *Seven Hundred Years of Oriental Carpets* (1970; originally published in German, 1966). Later works include P.R.J. Ford, *Oriental Carpet Design: A Guide to Traditional Motifs, Patterns, and Symbols*, rev. ed. (1989); Leonard Michael Helfgott, *Ties That Bind: A Social History of the Iranian Carpet* (1994); Daniel S. Walker, *Flowers Underfoot: Indian Carpets of the Mughal Era* (1997), an exhibition catalogue; John Train, *Oriental Rug Symbols: Their Origins and Meanings from the Middle East to China* (1997); Volkmar Gantzhorn, *Oriental Carpets: Their Iconology and Iconography, from Earliest Times to the 18th Century* (1998); John B. Gregorian, *Oriental Rugs of the Silk Route: Culture, Process, and Selection* (2000); and Jennifer Mary Wearden, *Oriental Carpets and Their Structure: Highlights from the V&A Collection* (2003).

EARLY PERIOD

Most of the issues scholars address relating to Islamic arts are summarized in Oleg Grabar, *The Formation of Islamic Art* (1973). Other useful works on architecture are K.A.C. Creswell, *A Short Account of*

Early Muslim Architecture (1989), revised and enlarged by James W. Allan; and R.W. Hamilton, *Khirbat al-Mafjar: An Arabian Mansion in the Jordan Valley* (1959).

Middle Period

Two valuable books on Fāṭimid art are Anna Contadini, *Fatimid Art at the Victoria and Albert Museum* (1998); and *Book of Gifts and Rarities* (1996), attributed to al-Rashīd ibn al-Zubayr, trans. and with notes by Ghāda al-Ḥijjāwī al-Qaddūmī. Works on the Seljuqs include Doğan Kuban, *The Miracle of Divriği: An Essay on the Art of Islamic Ornamentation in Seljuk Times* (2001; originally published in Turkish). Two excellent volumes on the Alhambra are Robert Irwin, *The Alhambra* (2004); and Oleg Grabar, *The Alhambra,* 2nd ed., rev. (1992). Esin Atil, *Renaissance of Islam* (1981), is a comprehensive study of Mamlūk art. Mongol arts are discussed in Donald N. Wilber, *The Architecture of Islamic Iran: The Il Khānid Period* (1955, reprinted 1969); and M.Ş. İpşiroğlu, *Painting and Culture of the Mongols* (1966; originally published in German, 1965). Timurid architecture is treated in Lisa Golombek and Donald N. Wilber, *The Timurid Architecture of Iran and Turan*, 2 vol. (1988); and Lisa Golombek, *The Timurid Shrine at Gazur Gah* (1969). Paintings are the focus of Ernst J. Grube, *The Classical Style in Islamic Painting* (1968); and illustrations are the subject of Oleg Grabar and Sheila Blair, *Epic Images and Contemporary History: The Illustrations of the Great Mongol Shahnama* (1980). Late Period

Esin Atil, *The Age of Sultan Süleyman the Magnificent* (1987), is an exhibition catalogue. Ottoman architecture is treated in Doğan Kuban, *Ottoman Architecture* (2010; originally published in Turkish, 2007), trans. by Adair Mill; and Gülru Necipoglu, *The Age of Sinan: Architectural Culture in the Ottoman Empire* (2005). Godfrey Goodwin, *A History of Ottoman Architecture* (1971) and Aptullah Kuran, *The Mosque in Early Ottoman Architecture* (1968), are older standard works on Ottoman architecture. Painting is covered in Wendy M.K. Shaw, *Ottoman Painting: Reflections of Western Art from the Ottoman Empire to the Turkish Republic* (2011) and Nurhan Atasoy and Filiz Çağman, *Turkish Miniature Painting* (1974).

Ṣafavid art and architecture are discussed in Sheila R. Canby, *Shah ʿAbbas: The Remaking of Iran* (2009), an exhibition catalog from the British Museum; Jon Thompson and Sheila R. Canby (eds.), *Hunt for Paradise: Court Arts of Safavid Iran, 1501–1576* (2003); Sheila R. Canby (ed.), *Safavid Art and Architecture* (2002); Kishwar Rizvi, *The Safavid Dynastic Shrine: Architecture, Religion, and Power in Early Modern Iran* (2011); Donald N. Wilber, *Persian Gardens and Garden Pavilions*, 2nd ed. (1979); Renata Holod (ed.), *Studies on Isfahan* (1974); Eugenio Galdieri, *Eṣfahān, ʿAli Qāpū: An Architectural Survey* (1979); Martin Bernard Dickson and Stuart C. Welch (eds.), *The Houghton Shahnameh* (1981); and Anthony Welch, *Artists for the Shah: Late Sixteenth-Century Painting at the Imperial Court of Iran* (1976).

Contemporary architecture in the developing world was the focus of the quarterly journal *Mimar* (1981–92), published in Singapore; it was the first periodical of its kind.

SPAIN

Works that treat Islamic influence in Spain include Jerrilynn D. Dodds (ed.), *Al-Andalus: The Art of Islamic Spain* (1992), an exhibition catalogue; Jerrilynn D. Dodds, *Architecture and Ideology in Early Medieval Spain* (1990); Salma Khadra Jayyusi (ed.), *The Legacy of Muslim Spain*, 2nd ed. (1994, reprinted 2000); Heather Ecker, *Caliphs and Kings: The Art and Influence of Islamic Spain* (2004); Shahid Suhrawardy, *The Art of the Mussulmans in Spain* (2005); and Mariam

Rosser-Owen, *Islamic Arts from Spain* (2010).

Anatolia

A study focused on a specific period is Raymond Lifchez (ed.), *The Dervish Lodge: Architecture, Art, and Sufism in Ottoman Turkey* (1992). Other sources on this region include Oktay Aslanapa, *Turkish Art and Architecture*, 2nd ed. (2004); Esin Atil (ed.), *Turkish Art* (1980); Yanni Petsopoulos (ed.), Tulips, *Arabesques & Turbans: Decorative Arts from the Ottoman Empire* (1982); and Ekrem Akurgal (ed.), *The Art and Architecture of Turkey* (1980).

Iran

Nothing has superseded Arthur Upham Pope and Phyllis Ackerman (eds.), *A Survey of Persian Art from Prehistoric Times to the Present,* 16 vol., 3rd ed. (1977–99), with two supplemental volumes, edited by Abbas Daneshvari and Jay Gluck, issued in 2005. Also helpful is R.W. Ferrier (ed.), *The Arts of Persia* (1989). A concise account of two centuries of Persian art is Sheila R. Canby, *The Golden Age of Persian Art: 1501–1722* (1999). An accounting of little-known Persian art found in former Soviet institutions is Vladimir Loukonine and Anatoli Ivanov, *Lost Treasures of Persia: Persian Art in the Hermitage Museum* (1996; originally published in Russian; also published as *Persian Art*). Important information is to be found in Hans E. Wulff, *The Traditional Crafts of Persia* (1966); and in Arthur Upham Pope, *Persian Architecture: The Triumph of Form and Color* (1965), and other works by the same author.

India

A good introduction is the second volume of J.C. Harle, *The Art and Architecture of the Indian Subcontinent*, 2nd ed. (1994). Among the best of several architectural surveys are Percy Brown, *Indian Architecture*, vol. 2, *The Islamic Period*, 6th reprint ed. (1975); and Satish Grover, *Islamic Architecture in India*, 2nd ed. (2002). Also useful are R. Nath, *History of Sultanate Architecture* (1978), and *History of Mughal Architecture* (1982); Stuart C. Welch, *The Art of Mughal India* (1963, reprinted 1976); Elizabeth B. Moynihan, *Paradise as a Garden* (1979); Milo Cleveland Beach, *The Imperial Image: Paintings for the Mughal Court*, rev. and expanded ed. (2012); *Mughal and Rajput Painting* (1992, reprinted 2000); and Som Prakash Verma, *Painting the Mughal Experience* (2005).

INDEX

A

ʿAbbāsid dynasty, 21–22, 35, 37, 38–39, 40, 50, 55, 58, 70
Alhambra palace, 77–79
Amazigh/Imazighen (Berber) dynasties, 53, 76–77
architecture
  assessment of in early Islamic period, 51–52
  building materials and technology, 40–43
  decoration, 43–47
  European influence on, 113–115
  Fāṭimid, 54–58
  Il-Khanid, 87–88
  Mamlūk, 82–84
  Moorish, 76–80
  of mosques, 23–31, 54–55
  Mughal, 105–107
  of other religious buildings, 31–34
  Ottoman, 95–98
  secular, 34–39
  Ṣafavid, 100–102
  Seljuq, 61–72
  Timurid, 88–89
  urban, 39–40

B

Baghdad, Iraq, 21, 34, 39, 40, 55, 63, 75, 86
book/manuscript illustration
  Fāṭimid, 59
  Mongol, 89–93
  Mughal, 107–111
  Ṣafavid, 102–103
  Seljuq, 73–75

C

calligraphy, 16, 60, 74, 80, 86
  Arabic script, 18–19
caravansaries, 40, 64–65, 66, 97, 100

D

Damascus, 21, 24, 25, 26–28, 34, 38, 44, 47, 62, 63, 70, 81, 82, 83, 98
Dome of the Rock, 30, 44

I

Il-Khan dynasty, 86–87
ivory carving
  early period, 49–50
  Moorish, 80
  Ottoman, 99

J

Jerusalem, 13, 24, 25, 26, 30, 41, 43, 44, 57, 81, 82, 84

M

madrasah, 34, 63, 66, 70, 71, 77, 82, 89, 95, 100
mausoleums
Fāṭimid, 55–57
Il-Khanid, 87
Mamlūks, 82–83
Moorish, 77
Mughal, 104, 106
Ottoman, 95
Sāmānids, 41
Seljuq, 62–63, 66–67, 68
Shīʿite influence on, 32–33
Timurid, 88–89
metalwork
early period, 50
Mamlūk, 81, 86
Moorish, 80
Ottoman, 99
Seljuq 73, 75–76
mosques
classic, 28–31
early constructions of, 23–25
Fāṭimid, 54–55, 57
hypostyle, 24, 25, 26, 28, 29, 30, 37, 42, 54, 55, 77, 82, 104
Il-Khanid, 87
Mamlūk, 82, 84
Moorish, 77
Mughal, 104, 105, 106, 107
origins of, 12–14
Ottoman, 95–97
Ṣafavid, 100
Seljuq, 62, 63, 65–66, 68, 70
three great, 25–28
Timurid, 88, 89
Mughal atelier, 109
Mughal Empire, 104
muqarnas, 43, 57, 58, 67, 70, 71, 79, 87, 89

O

Ottoman Empire, 94–95

P

painting, 8
early period, 17, 43, 44, 48, 49
Fāṭimid, 57–58, 59
Mongol, 89–93
Mughal, 104, 107–113
Ottoman, 98
Ṣafavid, 99, 102–104
Seljuq, 69, 72, 73
pottery/ceramics
early period, 43, 47–49, 51
Fāṭimid, 59–61
Moorish, 80
Ottoman, 98
Seljuq, 73, 75, 76

Q

qiblah, 12, 23, 24, 25, 26, 27, 28, 30, 31, 66, 84

R

ribāṭ, 31, 32, 63, 65, 82

S

Ṣafavid dynasty, 99–100
stucco
  early period, 43, 46
  Fāṭimid, 57, 58
  Mamlūk, 84
  Moorish, 77, 79
  Ṣafavid, 101
  Seljuq, 68–69
  Timurid, 89

T

textiles, 8, 9
  early period, 50, 51
  Moorish, 80
  Ottoman, 99
  Ṣafavid, 103
  Seljuq, 73
Timurid dynasty, 86–87

U

Umayyad dynasty, 21, 22, 25, 26, 35, 36, 37, 38, 43, 44, 47, 49, 70

V

visual arts
  assessment of in early Islamic period, 51–52
  decorative, 47–50
  earlier artistic traditions influencing, 11–12
  European influence on, 113–115
  Fāṭimid, 58–61
  Mamlūk, 84–86
  Mongol, 89–93
  Moorish, 80–81
  Mozarabic, 80–81
  Mudéjar, 80
  Mughal, 107–113
  Ottoman, 98–99
  prohibition against images in, 14–20
  Ṣafavid, 102–104
  Seljuq, 73–76